P9-DCO-471

Discussions that Work

CAMBRIDGE HANDBOOKS FOR LANGUAGE TEACHERS
General Editors: Michael Swan and Roger Bowers

This is a series of practical guides for teachers of English and other languages. Illustrative examples are usually drawn from the field of English as a foreign or second language, but the ideas and techniques described can equally well be used in the teaching of any language.

In this series:

Drama Techniques in Language Learning – A resource book of communication activities for language teachers
by Alan Maley and Alan Duff

Games for Language Learning
by Andrew Wright, David Betteridge and Michael Buckby

Discussions that Work – Task-centred fluency practice *by Penny Ur*

Once Upon a Time – Using stories in the language classroom
by John Morgan and Mario Rinvolucri

Teaching Listening Comprehension *by Penny Ur*

Keep Talking – Communicative fluency activities for language teaching
by Friederike Klippel

Working with Words – A guide to teaching and learning vocabulary
by Ruth Gairns and Stuart Redman

Learner English – A teacher's guide to interference and other problems
edited by Michael Swan and Bernard Smith

Testing Spoken Language – A handbook of oral testing techniques
by Nic Underhill

Literature in the Language Classroom – A resource book of ideas and activities
by Joanne Collie and Stephen Slater

Discussions that Work

Task-centred fluency practice

Penny Ur

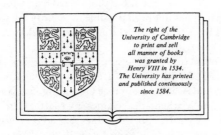

The right of the
University of Cambridge
to print and sell
all manner of books
was granted by
Henry VIII in 1534.
The University has printed
and published continuously
since 1584.

Cambridge University Press
Cambridge
New York   New Rochelle
Melbourne   Sydney

Published by the Press Syndicate of the University of Cambridge
The Pitt Building, Trumpington Street, Cambridge CB2 1RP
32 East 57th Street, New York, NY 10022, USA
10 Stamford Road, Oakleigh, Melbourne 3166, Australia

© Cambridge University Press 1981

First published 1981
Eighth printing 1988

Printed in Great Britain
at the University Press, Cambridge

British Library cataloguing in publication data

Ur, Penny

Discussions that work. – (Cambridge handbooks for language teachers.
New series)
1. English language – Spoken English
2. English language – Study and teaching –
Foreign students
I. Title
428.2'4   PE1128   80-42199

ISBN 0 521 28169 5

Acknowledgements

The author would like to thank Harold Fish of the University of
Birmingham and Dalia Goldberg of Kfar Menachem, Israel for their ideas
which have been incorporated into this book.

The author and publishers are grateful to those listed below for permission
to reproduce material. It has not been possible to identify the sources of
all the material used and in such cases the publishers would welcome
information from copyright owners.
Young and Rubicam Ltd (fig. 2b); Dominic Sansoni (fig. 2c); Françoise
Grellet (figs. 2d, 3a, 3b, 3c, 3d); *Pictorial Education* (fig. 4a); Longman
Group Ltd (fig. 4b); Sun Alliance Insurance Group (fig. 5a); *Scientific
American* (fig. 5b, from 'Mathematical Games' by Martin Gardner,
copyright © 1980 by Scientific American, Inc. All rights reserved);
Punch (fig. 5c); the poem on p. 67 is from *By the Waters of Manhattan* by
Charles Reznikoff, copyright © 1959 by Charles Reznikoff. Reprinted by
permission of New Directions Publishing Corporation.
    The drawings in figs. 2a, 5d, 6, 7 and 8 are by Chris Evans. Fig. 4d was
drawn by Jenny Palmer.

Contents

Preface   1

Part 1: General principles   2

What is a discussion?   2
Communication practice   2
The discussion   2
The aims   3
A discussion that works   3

Some factors in a good discussion: topic, group-work, role-play   5
The topic   5
Group-work   7
Role-play   9

Giving the discussion a purpose: the task   12
Thought   13
Result   13
Language-practice efficiency   13
Simplicity   14
Preparation   14
Interaction   15
Interest   15

Organization   18
Presentation   18
Process   18
Ending   22
Feedback   22
Conclusion   24

Part 2: Practical examples 25

Introduction   25

Brainstorming activities   27
1   Guessing games   27
2   Finding connections   33
3   Ideas from a central theme   35
4   Implications and interpretations   39

Organizing activities   48
5   Comparing   48
6   Detecting differences   51
7   Putting in order   60
8   Priorities   67
9   Choosing candidates (a)   73
10   Choosing candidates (b)   79
11   Layout problems   80
12   Combining versions   90

Compound activities   98
13   Composing letters   98
14   Debates   105
15   Publicity campaigns   108
16   Surveys   111
17   Planning projects   112

Bibliography   119
Index   122

Preface

This book deals with one particular aspect of the teaching of English as a foreign language: fluency practice. It suggests some ways in which students may be induced to *talk* in the classroom, using the language creatively, purposefully and individually. The vehicle of such use is defined as the *discussion*, in a very broad sense of the word. In Part 1, I have tried to isolate and generalize about a number of elements that are essential for a good discussion; some of these are well-known and have been extensively written about (interesting topics, group-work, role-play), while others have been relatively neglected (the task as focus, organization of process). Part 2 consists of practical examples of discussion activities. These are directly or indirectly based on exercises I have actually tried and found effective.

Many of the ideas are more relevant to the teaching of students who are reasonably proficient in English, i.e. intermediate and more advanced classes in language institutes and universities and the upper classes of secondary schools. Some of them however can be used successfully with elementary and lower-intermediate classes and I have indicated this where relevant.

At the end of the book can be found a *Bibliography* and an *Index*. The *Bibliography* is selective; its purpose is to suggest further reading that may assist the teacher in the planning, preparation and execution of classroom discussions; books and articles are presented under subject-headings rather than alphabetically, with brief comments on their content and use. The *Index* is simply an alphabetical list of all the activities described in this book.

One further note: I have referred to the teacher throughout in the feminine. This is not because I have anything against men teachers, but because I, and the vast majority of English teachers of my acquaintance, are women.

Part 1: General principles

What is a discussion?

Communication practice

Much of our time as language teachers is taken up teaching
particular features of phonology, lexis or structure: presenting
them, getting students to practise them, testing them and so on.
But when our students have (we hope) learnt them, we have
the problem of getting them to use their knowledge for actual
purposeful verbal communication. This side of language teaching
has come into greater prominence in recent years; instead of the
idea, associated with the audio–lingual school, that students
should use language in more or less controlled exercises until they
have mastered its structures to a high degree, and only then
begin to talk freely, it is now accepted that some sort of dynamic,
individual and meaningful oral practice should be included in
English lessons right from the beginning. And if this is seen as
important at the early stages – how much more so at the
advanced! Most courses now emphasize the importance of
fostering learners' ability to *communicate* in the foreign language
rather than their skill in constructing correct sentences, and there
is a corresponding increase in the time and energy allotted to
communication exercises in the classroom.

It is, however, worth noting here that if communication
practice is one of the most important components of the language
learning/teaching process, it is also one of the most problematical.
It is much more difficult to get learners to express themselves
freely than it is to extract right answers in a controlled exercise.

The discussion

The most natural and effective way for learners to practise talking
freely in English is by thinking out some problem or situation
together through verbal interchange of ideas; or in simpler terms,
to *discuss*. I am using the word 'discussion' here rather broadly
to include anything from the simplest question–answer guessing
process, through exploration of situations by role-play, to the
most complex political and philosophical debates; I include

2

not only the talking but also any reading and writing that may be entailed.

The aims

The main aim of a discussion in a foreign language course may be *efficient fluency practice,* but it is by no means the only one; indeed, it cannot be, by definition. It is today commonplace to say that language is never used (except in the classroom) for its own sake, but always for the sake of achieving an objective, or to perform a function: to persuade, inform, inquire, threaten, etc. Language, in short, is always a means to an end; and we cannot expect proper use of the means if we do not supply a reasonable end. Hence *achieving an objective* in itself must form one of our aims in holding discussions. As language teachers, we may see this as more or less secondary, but never negligible; and for our students at least it should be the central thought focus during talking. The purpose of the discussion, whether it is solving a problem, exploring the implications of an idea, constructing proposals or whatever, is to be taken very seriously and the results respected by teacher and students alike.

Learning from content may be a third aim; in many discussions there is much to be learnt from what is said: information may be acquired, for example, or new points of view considered.

Finally, we may wish to foster another kind of learning: learning how to participate constructively and cooperatively in a discussion. This involves *clear, logical thought* on the one hand and *debating skills* on the other. By clear, logical thought I mean things like the ability to generalize from examples, or the converse, to draw analogies, judge priorities, infer causes and so on. Debating skills include listening to what someone else has to say, not interrupting, speaking relevantly and clearly.

A discussion that works

For our purposes, a discussion that works is primarily one in which as many students as possible say as much as possible. I am not denying that aural comprehension is as important as speaking – or more so – but listening can be done by all the class simultaneously, whereas only a limited number of students can talk at one time; and talking, therefore, is liable to be practised less.

A further characteristic of a successful discussion is the apparent motivation of the participants: if I look around and see

3

that all those not actually speaking are concentrating their attention on the speaker(s), and that their expressions are alive, that they are reacting to the humour, seriousness or difficulty of the ideas being expressed – then that is another sign that things are going well.

If, finally, I can discern both these symptoms – full participation and high motivation – in a series of discussion exercises where language is used in a variety of ways in terms of subject-matter and communicative functions, then I have reason to be pleased with my class and with myself.

Some factors in a good discussion: topic, group-work, role-play

The topic

Its necessity

The problem of getting students to express themselves freely in the foreign language has come into prominence in recent years as a result of the growing emphasis on communicative abilities. But the basic idea of encouraging fluency through conversation is as old as language teaching itself. One conventional way of doing this is the 'conversation class', where a group of students sit down with a teacher – a native speaker if they are lucky – and are required to talk with her. This often degenerates into a more or less biographical question-and-answer session of the where-do-you-live-what-are-your-hobbies variety, monopolized by the minority of fluent speakers. The reason for this is in the first place the lack of a defined and interesting *topic*.

So the first thing to do is to bring interesting subjects of conversation to the classroom. Teachers increasingly hold topic-centred discussions or debates as a framework for fluency practice, and many books for use in the classroom have been published to help them think of suitable subjects (see *Bibliography*). Such exercises are often successful; at any rate, they are a vast improvement on the unstructured conversation class.

Topic is still seen by most teachers as the central focus of classroom discussions. To my mind, it is certainly important, but not central: the crux is not *what* to talk about, but *why* you need to talk about it; of this, more later.

Limitations

Now a discussion which has no aim but to discuss the topic may, and often does, succeed, if the students are the type that enjoys arguing and are able to think in abstractions. But often, in my experience, the participation gradually subsides until you hear the familiar cry: 'I can't think of anything to say!' What the students who say this actually mean is that they *have no reason* to say anything. To tell students to talk about abortion, or the latest political scandal, or whatever, is almost as bad as telling them simply to talk English. Why should they? They would never, outside the classroom, dream of inventing sentences about a subject merely for the sake of speaking. Such speech only imitates real conversation, it is in truth as artificial as most other classroom exercises, for it lacks the *purpose* of genuine discourse; and from this lack of purpose springs the lack of interest and motivation that too often leads to the 'petering out' phenomenon. In short, students need a *reason* to speak more than they need something to speak *about;* once they have such a reason, however, the fact that the topic is stimulating will make the whole discussion more interesting.

The topics themselves, moreover, are often rather limited. Most teachers and materials-writers mistakenly treat the concept 'interesting' as somehow synonymous with 'controversial', and 'discussion' as the same as 'argument'. Most of our normal talking is concerned with subjects that are more or less interesting to us, but few of them are actually controversial, and very little of our talking is arguing. If we want our discussions to give the students practice in a varied sample of language functions, then we must considerably widen our conception of what makes an interesting subject. The best illustration of what I mean will be supplied by a quick glance through some of the examples given in Part 2.

Further reservations I have about solely topic-centred discussions concern the usual manner of their organization. Firstly, in proposing a subject for debate, teachers (or their books) often misguidedly make their students a present of all the main arguments and items of information they are likely to need, thus robbing them of the initiative. Half the fun of debating is thinking up cogent points, bringing fresh evidence, or suggesting original examples. If all this has been done for them, then all the students can do (unless they are very original) is paraphrase ready-made ideas. These are unlikely to interest either speaker or listener, and we are back to the problem of lack of purpose.

Secondly, such discussions are nearly always carried out in the full class forum, a group of anything from fifteen to forty students. Now as I said before, we want all our students to speak, and for as much time as possible; the simplest arithmetic will make it clear that in a forty-minute period, even if every member of the class speaks, he will do so for only a minute or two; not one's idea of optimum active learner participation. Of course, in reality even this is not achieved. The discussion is usually dominated by a few fluent speakers, and the rest either listen, or, bored by being passive bystanders, lose interest completely and turn to some other occupation, which may or may not have a disrupting influence on the proceedings!

Group-work

Organization

The obvious answer to the problem raised at the end of the last
section is to divide the class into discussion groups of between
two and eight participants. In fact, this is so obvious that it is
surprising how little it is done. It took me some time to reach this
conclusion myself, partly because I simply never thought of it
(so naturally does one teach by the methods by which one
was taught!), and partly because, having thought of it, I was a
little apprehensive of trying it, afraid of the lack of discipline that
would result from the sheer physical reorganization of the
classroom and from the decentralization of the teaching process.
However, these problems turned out to be far from insuperable.
The physical reorganization can be done very simply by getting
some students to turn to face those behind them if they are
normally in rows. This may need a little modification to ensure
that groups are heterogeneous – or homogeneous, if that is more
suitable to the exercise – and that there are no serious personality
clashes; but once the students are settled into fixed groups, they
will assume them quickly and with little fuss each time. Chopping
and changing groups each session may sometimes produce
restlessness and indiscipline, at least in younger classes; in such
cases, it is best to make the groups semi-permanent.

Advantages

The first advantage of group-work is of course the increased
participation. If you have five or six groups then there will be five
or six times the amount of talking. Class discussions, as has been
pointed out, are very wasteful in terms of the ratio of teacher-
or student-effort and time to actual language practice taking place;
group discussions are relatively efficient. Moreover, this
heightened participation is not limited to those who are usually
articulate anyway; students who are shy of saying something
in front of the whole class, or to the teacher, often find it much
easier to express themselves in front of a small group of their
peers.
    The motivation of participants also improves when they work
in small groups. This is partly a function of the release from
inhibition described above, but other factors also play a part. The
physical focus of the discussion is close and directed towards the
individual student; that is to say, whoever is speaking is only a
small distance away, clearly audible, facing the others and

addressing them personally. Any visual or other materials are likewise close by: the whole activity is immediate and 'involving'. More important, group-work lends itself to game-like activities; almost any task-centred exercise can be transformed into a game by adding an element of tension. Where this is not supplied by the task itself, the simple institution of an arbitrary time-limit or inter-group competition can easily do so.

Another advantage of group-work is that it frees the teacher from her usual role of instructor–corrector–controller, and allows her to wander freely round the class, giving help where needed, assessing the performance of individual students, noting language mistakes for future remedial work, devoting a little more time to slower learners. She also has an important role to play in leading and encouraging discussions (see *Organization*).

Finally, there is scope here for peer-teaching. In the course of group discussions, students will learn from each other, whether consciously or unconsciously. They may correct each other's mistakes, help out with a needed word; and of course they will teach each other some non-linguistic material as well, through the content of the discussion.

Problems

There are various problems associated with group-work. Don't students get out of control? Don't they tend to lapse into their native language when not under the teacher's eye? Isn't the organization into groups time-consuming, noisy and disruptive? What do you do with students who won't take part? Or with a group that finishes too early? How do you draw the session to a close? And so on. These questions have to do partly with that nebulous quality called 'discipline', partly with practical organization. As regards discipline: this basically depends on the personality of the teacher, her class, and the relationship between them, not on the type of activity. On the whole it is safe to say that a class which is controlled in frontal work will be controlled also in groups. Thoughtful and efficient organization can, however, contribute a good deal to solving the problems enumerated above. The subject of the physical division of the class has been dealt with at the beginning of this section; others will be gone into more fully in the section on *Organization*.

Role-play

What it is

Giving students a suitable *topic* provides interest and subject-matter for discussion, dividing them into *groups* improves the amount and quality of the verbal interaction. *Role-play,* though perhaps a little less important, can add a significant dimension to the 'standard' discussion, and is today more and more widely used.

For role-play, the class is usually divided into small groups – often pairs – which are given situations and roles to act out and explore. This acting is done for the sake of the language and imaginative activity, not for exhibition; though students may occasionally enjoy seeing or showing off some particularly successful scene. The various groups, therefore, are activated simultaneously. They may be standing or sitting, static or moving. Mime may also be involved.

Advantages

The use of role-play has added a tremendous number of possibilities for communication practice. Students are no longer limited to the kind of language used by learners in a classroom: they can be shopkeepers or spies, grandparents or children, authority figures or subordinates; they can be bold or frightened, irritated or amused, disapproving or affectionate; they can be in Buckingham Palace or on a ship or on the moon; they can be threatening, advising, apologizing, condoling. The language can correspondingly vary along several parameters: according to the profession, status, personality, attitudes or mood of the character being role-played, according to the physical setting imagined, according to the communicative functions or purpose required. At one stroke, the limits of language use are enormously widened.

Moreover, role-play exercises are usually based on real-life situations: hence the speech they require is close to genuine discourse, and provides useful practice in the kinds of language the learners may eventually need to use in similar situations outside the classroom.

Many students find this type of practice easier and more attractive than ordinary discussion. There are various reasons for this. Firstly, the fact that the kind of speech involved is concrete and personal, the issues relevant to actual life, make it relatively easy to think of things to say. Secondly, the criteria of what are 'good things to say' are no longer so intellectual; the student

does not have to say anything clever or original; any utterances
that are true to the situation are acceptable, he can express himself
in exclamations or half-sentences, he can repeat himself –
anything goes (almost)! Hence it is much easier for the student to
be successful, and his confidence and self-esteem are boosted.
Thirdly, many students find it easier to express themselves from
behind the mask of being someone else; others find it simply more
stimulating and exciting.

Limitations

Role-play exercises, with a teacher who likes them and believes in
their potential, and with a reasonably uninhibited class, can
show excellent results. But even the most apparently attractive
activities often do not work. Sometimes this is because there
is too much mime involved and little efficient language practice.
But even when the exercise is all speech-oriented, students
may find it difficult to get going, and when they do, the talking
often 'peters out' after a few exchanges, and we are back to:
'I've got nothing to say!'
There are two major problems here, one concerned with the
nature of role-play itself, and one with a dimension missing from
many such exercises. The first is the problem of student
inhibition. Many students, unused to this type of exercise,
particularly more mature ones with a non-Western-cultural
background, find it difficult to pretend to be someone else. The
result is often embarrassment and an unwillingness to participate,
expressed in scorn ('Let's stop these childish games and have a
real lesson!'), giggling, or slow, forced conversations which grind
to a halt fairly quickly. This problem can be overcome by
unremitting efforts on the part of a dedicated teacher, coupled
with explanations of what she is trying to do; but in some
situations it may not be worth the effort.
The second problem brings me yet again to the question of
purpose. In most role-play exercises, students are given a stimulus-
situation and/or roles, but they are given no final objective to
aim for. The situation is left open to them to interpret and
develop as they see fit. Now in a successful exercise of this kind,
this is what will in fact happen. All sorts of interesting conflicts
and ramifications will come up, which the students will react
to spontaneously, getting more and more involved and interested,
acting more and more convincingly – for of course the original
function of such activities was to develop acting ability, not
language. But put into a foreign language learning context, this
lack of specific direction and purpose sometimes results rather in

confusion and uncertainty what to do next; partly because our students are not all relaxed and imaginative enough, partly because they are relatively limited in their technical ability to express themselves.

Role-play is a step up from 'talk about x'; it is now 'talk about x in role-situation y'; but we need one final step: 'talk about x in role-situation y *in order to achieve z*'.

Giving the discussion a purpose: the task

When a group is given a *task* to perform through verbal interaction, all speech becomes purposeful, and therefore more interesting. I should like to illustrate this by describing a short series of lessons I once gave in an 'oral English' course. The class was composed of future English-teachers who were not native speakers. I asked one of the students to organize a discussion on the kind of subject she thought might be relevant to adolescent pupils. She suggested parent–child relationships. Asked to be more specific, she invited the class to express their opinions on over-possessive mothers. One or two students volunteered isolated generalized opinions, but the discussion did not 'flow'. I suggested that the student organizer go away and come back next week with some more concrete focus for debate. She returned with a dialogue between three children, complaining about their parents, which she read out. This was better: the students related to the three situations and commented on them. But the discussion still lacked direction and did not last long. I then took her dialogue home with me, selected one of the three situations she had invented, and composed letters to a women's magazine 'help and advice' column: one from a daughter complaining about her mother, the other from the mother. I divided the fourteen-strong class into two groups, gave one of the letters to each, and set them to compose answers, in the capacity of the editors of the column. This time the discussion was enthusiastic and I had to stop it before it finished as we ran out of time. The necessity to actually formulate reasonable, tactful and helpful answers (the task) forced the participants to delve deeply and carefully into the problems involved; and, through the particular case, they found themselves discussing general values and sources of conflict. It was then, I suppose, that I realized the vital difference that the 'task' element makes to a discussion.

In Part 2 of this book are many examples of actual tasks (the texts of the letters used in the exercise described above can be found, slightly adapted, in *Composing letters,* p. 98); here I shall only set out some of the theoretical factors to be considered when devising them.

12

Thought

Language use implies thought; and a task involving talking must also involve thinking out. Standing on one's head, for example, may constitute a task, but it has nothing to do with language unless and until student A has to think how to get student B to stand on his head; he could, if he is strong enough, turn him upside down(!), but on the whole it is more convenient to give instructions. Here, the thinking – as it often does – involves an aspect of problem-solving: in this case, how to get someone else to do what you want; and its most simple and obvious implication is the use of speech.

The kinds of thinking involved can be described in terms of logical relationships and processes: generalization, exemplification, analysis, synthesis, evaluation, contrast, analogy, comparison, priority, cause, reason, purpose, result, inference, implication, interpretation, summary, amplification, alternativity. This is by no means a definitive list of possible thinking processes, but it is a fair selection; and I have found many of the categories of practical use as bases for the construction of discussion tasks.

Result

Each task consists of a thinking process and its outcome in the form of a tangible result. It is not enough just to think out a problem or explore the ramifications of a conflict: the results must be written down, ticked off, listed, sketched, or tape-recorded in some way – some kind of conclusion must be set down in a form that can be presented to the teacher and the rest of the class. This serves several purposes. Firstly, it focuses and defines what the group has to do; it constitutes the end product of the talking. Secondly, it provides a clear signal that the group has finished; there is no excuse for saying 'we've finished' before completing the task, or for uncertainty or disagreement between participants as to whether they have in fact completed what they set out to do. Thirdly, it provides a basis for *feedback,* an important aspect of the administration of such discussions, which I shall come on to in the section on *Organization.*

Language-practice efficiency

Of course, we as teachers have our own task in these exercises: we want to set up optimum conditions for our students to talk to each other. We must, therefore, be rather careful about the kind of task we set. We must have one eye on the clock and one on the kind of activity the students are doing, with a constant awareness of the relationship between the two. Miming, for example, is an attractive basis for conjecture and interpretation, but sometimes too much time can be spent on intricate mime with relatively little speech. Or problem-solving, again a good stimulus for talking, can sometimes be accompanied by long pauses for puzzling out, not directly entailing language use. It is unfortunately rather easy to allow oneself to be caught up by enthusiasm for absorbing and original group tasks whose efficiency in affording opportunity for language practice is minimal.

Simplicity

On the whole, the simpler the task, the more chance it has of success. If it is too complex, valuable discussion time will be wasted on teacher-explanations, and there is a danger that groups may lose the thread of what they are doing, or misunderstand. The teacher may, of course, set a very easily explained task which involves rather complicated discussion-procedure; however, as long as this is student-initiated, and they know what they are doing, it does not matter. The main point is that the final aim should be sufficiently simple to be clear to participants at all stages.

Preparation

The task should be simple from the teacher's point of view as well: that is, it should be simple to prepare. An activity with a great deal of complex preparation in terms of typing, duplicating, recording or the use of elaborate aids may well be successful – if it ever takes place! For many teachers, the necessity for this sort of preparation is, if not prohibitive, at least severely discouraging. We may manage to prepare two or three, or even half a dozen such exercises a year; but this is insufficient for effective fluency practice. In general, we shall only be able to hold discussion activities at regular and frequent intervals if we can limit their preparation to the less-than-one-hour's period usually available for the purpose. An occasional free day or burst of energy may enable us to do more; but this must remain the exception, not the rule.

Interaction

It may sound superfluous to say that the task must entail interaction, yet it is very easy to set a task that fulfils all the other conditions I have mentioned, only to find that it can be much more easily performed by each student alone, and that this is probably what will in fact happen. One very entertaining task, for example, is to make up a story that has to include a number of totally incongruous words or expressions. The first time I set this, I found that students were either splitting off and producing individual stories, or letting one bright spark do all the work for the whole group. I solved this the next time by building in an organizational process that forced participants to interact: each one got only one of the words, and, as it came round to his turn, had to continue the story in such a way as to bring in his word (see p. 21).

Most open-ended tasks, however, lend themselves to interaction (by 'open-ended' I mean tasks requiring the gathering or proposing of ideas unlimited by one predetermined 'right' result). This is because the imaginative resources of a group are always greater than those of only one student, whereas the intellectual resources may not be; and the task will obviously be more easily and better performed by exploiting them. A convergent or 'closed-ended' problem is intrinsically less likely to be effective in that the moment one member of the group lights on the right answer (if it is obvious that it is right), there is an end to interaction. This may, however, continue if nobody knows whether the suggested answer is right or not, and there is room for argument.

Interest

To say that a language-learning activity should be interesting is, again, stating the obvious. Student motivation and performance are dependent to a large extent on the interest and enjoyment generated by the activity. But it may be worth dwelling a little on what exactly makes a task interesting.

The first essential component is the challenge of performing *the task itself*. If a task is too difficult, the group is discouraged before it begins; if too easy, students are quickly bored. There has to be a combination of challenge and ensured success: the task must be hard enough to demand an effort on the part of the group members, but easy enough for it to be clear that success is within their grasp. This is another reason for preferring open-ended tasks: they are success-oriented. However much or little is produced, whatever responses are given, it all constitutes a performance that may be more or less successful, but is unlikely to be a failure.

As regards interesting *subject-matter,* there are two schools of thought. One claims that the closer discussion material or role-play situations are to the students' own circumstances, the more interested they will be; and the other, that the more imaginative and exotic the subject, the more excited and stimulated the participants. Both theories have truth, as do the converse arguments: if the subject-matter is too far removed from students' own lives, they may find difficulty in understanding and manipulating it, whereas if it is too close to home they may be bored. Of course this dichotomy is only apparent, and springs, I think, from too imprecise a use of the word 'subject'. The subject consists of two things: a basic conflict or problem, which can be expressed in more or less abstract terms; and its expression in an actual context. What must be familiar to the students is the abstract framework: where or how it is realized is open to the imagination. For example, children are familiar from experience with the conflicts arising between authority-figures and subordinates (parent–child, teacher–pupil, etc.); they therefore have no difficulty in extrapolating to a situation of conflict between boss and workers, officers and men, warders and prisoners.

Role-play is another, optional, contributor to interest; its advantages and disadvantages in general have already been described. Many tasks can be done with or without role-play; (see for example *Choosing candidates,* p. 73).

There are one or two further elements which can add interest. The use of a *physical focus* for the discussion helps to keep students' attention centred on the subject and stimulate ideas. Object-based discussions (as in *Uses of an object,* p. 37) should always be done with the object physically present; pictures, graphic representations or relevant written details set before participants can also help to stimulate interest even if they are not strictly speaking essential to the understanding or performance of the task. *Writing down* results or ideas by one of the group members as the activity proceeds also helps to focus attention. Finally, as I have said elsewhere, group tasks are easily made into group *contests,* with an immediate rise in tension and motivation, and even so simple a stratagem as the setting of a *time-limit* has a similar effect.

Before leaving the subject of interest, I should like to add what may seem a rather odd reservation. This is that the discussion should not be made *too* interesting. It should be sufficiently absorbing to provide motivation to speak; but not so stimulating as to cause overheated debate, counter-productive to our language-learning and general educational aims. If students get so involved with their subject that they forget that they are in fact doing a serious learning exercise in a classroom, necessary self-restraints loosen: they may cease to let each other participate fairly, raise their voices and disturb other groups, laugh or dispute immoderately, and – worst of all from our point of view – drop for extended periods into their native language.

Organization

Now the task itself is of paramount importance; but very little less so is the manner of its administration. This may make all the difference between smooth, independent student performance and inefficient confusion.

Presentation

The presentation of the task should usually be made before any move is made by students to start work. I have often fallen into the trap of getting students into their groups, giving out the materials, and only then starting to explain what they have to do; by this time their attention is naturally focused on each other or on the materials, not on me, with a corresponding drop in concentration and comprehension. It is essential that the students should be completely clear in their minds right from the start what the task is, and what limitations are imposed on how they do it; hence they should be told this by the teacher while their attention is fully hers.

There is a limit, of course, to students' patience and concentration span; so the clearer and more concise the instructions the better. With classes whose knowledge of English is not yet up to understanding such instructions without a great deal of clarification and repetition, it may be most sensible to give these in the native language; time saved by giving the preliminary explanation in the vernacular is time gained for the discussion itself.

The first time a class does an activity, it is often a good idea to do a 'trial run', either with the full class, or using a group of good students as demonstrators. In the more lengthy discussions that involve a lot of negotiation and argument this is impractical and unnecessary; but in the shorter game-like activities it may be the best way to make sure that the rules and procedure are clear to all.

Process

If we want to ensure a smooth, efficient and enjoyable discussion we shall need to consider various aspects of its *process;* I use the

latter term to refer to *the way the discussion is held,* as distinct from
the *content of what is said.* Some of these aspects are points of
formal procedure, others are ad-hoc stratagems for dealing with
particular problems; some need to be included in the teacher's
preliminary instructions, others may only be put in during
the course of the talking. Not all the points mentioned in this
section are relevant to all discussions; but the teacher needs to be
aware of them and their possible application.

Firstly, how will the group set about the task? They may just
start talking, and often this is sufficient; but in some cases a
few simple refinements may make that talking much more
efficient and enjoyable. One is the *electing of functionaries* to do
particular jobs as the discussion proceeds; a chairman, for
example, or a secretary. Another is the organization of *strategy:*
what things are to be done in what order. In many creative or
interpretative exercises, for example, it is a good idea to start off
with a 'brainstorming' session, with the secretary noting down all
suggestions, preferably where they can be seen; and only then
start sifting and evaluating, rather than discussing each proposal as
it comes up. Or it may help for each participant to note down his
own ideas on the subject before the general discussion begins; or
for students to work in pairs first. Sometimes the introduction
of *game-rules* or other limitations can add zest; students may not be
allowed to see each other's materials, or may be limited in time
or media.

Another aspect of process which the teacher will do well to
consider before she starts is the *distribution of tasks.* In other words,
are all the groups going to do the same thing? Sometimes, if the
teacher can cope with the preparation and organization, groups
may do totally different exercises. But even where the groups are
all doing the same general type of activity, it is often a good
idea for the actual content of the tasks to be different; this stops
groups plagiarizing, and lowers the possibility of distraction. The
different tasks may be complementary (as in *Debates,* p. 105), or a
task completed by one group may be passed on to another (as in
Uses of an object, p. 37).

There are certain general *discussion skills,* also, about which the
teacher will need to remind her students. The need for reasonably
balanced participation of all members of the group, respect for
the chair, prohibition of interruptions, and even so simple a thing
as keeping voices down so as not to disturb other groups or
classes – all these may need to be consciously and systematically
taught, especially in younger classes. They may even be made
a part of the task, and the group's performance judged by
satisfactory standards in these aspects as well as by results.

The teacher may need to function discreetly as discussion leader in coping with specific problems as they come up. For example, it sometimes happens that the discussion gets rather involved, and there is a danger that participants may lose the thread of what is going on: it is very helpful for the teacher to step in with a *clarification* (if, of course, the number of groups is sufficiently small for her to be able to follow the developments in each). This may take the form of a simpler paraphrase of what has recently been said, or a summary of conclusions the group has already reached, or a redefinition of the problem in the light of new information or of a different viewpoint. Secondly, there is the *prevention of digressions*. Sometimes, it is true, digressions may take the form of interesting and possibly productive sidelines that can be left to develop; but the pointless, non-productive digression needs to be cut short, and it is up to the teacher, usually, to diagnose the difference and act accordingly. Thirdly, it may happen that the discussion flags or goes off the rails because of lack of ideas or too facile a treatment of the subject. Here the teacher may find herself making a *contribution to content*. In general, a good discussion-leader should concern herself with process only, but this has its exceptions. Contribution to content may in some cases prove the most effective oiler of the wheels of process. A suggestion from the teacher as to an alternative approach, or another contribution to the brainstorm, for instance, may give the whole debate a boost onwards. Or where the students have contented themselves with shallow, facile conclusions, have ignored inconvenient facts, or are over-biased, the teacher may very productively 'throw a spanner in the works': call to mind those unwelcome facts, or produce 'subversive' opinions (not necessarily her own!). All this tends to make the discussion more controversial and the treatment of the subject more thorough.

Other aspects of process are concerned with language practice. Firstly there is the question of the *discouragement of native language use*. The temptation to fall back on their native tongue is always before our students, and there is no one easy way to stop them succumbing. Exhortations and consistent reminders by the teacher help, but may not always be adequate. Stratagems which may be useful: if there is a group contest, then groups may be told that every occurrence of native-language use will lower their eventual score: the teacher cannot always be present to check this, so I have often found it effective to appoint an observer from among the students whose job it is to note any such transgression. Or you may put a tape-recorder (on 'record') by an offending group, and make sure they know about it – this is surprisingly effective.

Another problem connected with language use is *participation encouragement:* what can we do to ensure that all the students do have a chance to practise using the language actively? This can be built in to the task by such stratagems as the 'combining arrangement' (an idea based on the article of that name by I.S.P. Nation – see the *Bibliography*). What this means, basically, is that instead of giving all the data needed to solve a problem to the group as a whole, you give only one item to each member. Thus they all have to 'combine' (and therefore speak) in order to work out the answer (see for example the activity described on p. 15, or *Combining versions,* p. 90). Or we can insist that every student has to put forward at least one suggestion in a 'brainstorm'; this can be helped if a little time is allotted at the beginning for each student to think about or jot down his ideas. We can lay down that decisions must be made, if possible, by unanimous agreement rather than just majority vote (this has the added advantage that it makes the debate far more thorough). Alternatively, in an open-ended creative assignment, we can make it a condition that the result must contain at least one contribution from each group member.

What about *correcting mistakes* of language? Some teachers think this should never be done in fluency exercises, on the grounds that it is discouraging, interferes with the flow of discourse, and stops students having to make do with what they know. Now nothing, in my opinion, should 'never' or 'always' be done in language teaching (even this proposition probably has its exceptions!); such pronouncements are at best over-simplifications, at worst simply wrong. In the present case, there are reasons why one would want to compromise. Firstly, even if the teacher does not correct glaring errors, other students will, probably more rudely and less efficiently. Secondly, a student often knows he may be saying something wrong, or may simply not know how to say it at all, and will learn more from being given the appropriate form or item at a moment when he needs it to express himself, than he will from being forced to paraphrase. Lastly, withholding such help often hampers the discussion and discourages students more than giving it. However, the teacher is not always on the spot, and on such occasions the student will have plenty of practice in making do with the limited language available to him. In short, although we do not do formal language teaching in these activities, and though we want students to develop independence and fluency, there is a case for unobtrusive helping-out with specific errors or gaps as they come up.

Ending

How do we draw the discussions to a close? There are various problems here: one group may finish long before the others; all the groups may finish early, or be still fully absorbed far beyond the period previously estimated by the teacher.

Let us start with the first of these, as it comes up almost every time. The obvious answer is for the teacher to give the quickest group further work to do until all or most of the others finish. This further work may take the form of an elaboration of the task (You've made a list of possible items? Good, now put them in order of probability/priority/interest. You've made up your story? Now record it/prepare it for acting/write it out . . . and so on). The teacher may have self-access work-cards available for individual stop-gap occupation. Or she may simply say 'Get on with your homework' or 'Read your books'. In any case, these reserve occupations should be ready to hand; and their preparation is an essential part of the lesson plan as a whole.

At what point does one call a halt to the discussion? This is often difficult to gauge. Sometimes it may be best to wait until all the groups have completed the task, sometimes this takes too long, and it is better to stop the last ones before they finish; at other times it is even expedient to stop all groups while they are still absorbed and active, but have enough material ready to warrant a feeling of achievement and a fruitful feedback session. This last possibility has an added advantage: it leaves students with a taste for more, and thus with heightened enthusiasm, or at least willingness, for further such activities. A previously-given time-limit, of course, solves this problem at a stroke, but may not always be appropriate. Beyond these ideas, I can give no further reliable recommendations: it is up to the teacher to be flexible and rely on her common sense. However, one warning: if you think you may have to stop one or more groups before they finish, say so beforehand – this saves protests and delays when the time comes.

Feedback

The ending of the group discussions and the finishing of the task do not constitute the end of the exercise as a whole. It is not fair to students to ask them to put a lot of effort into something, and then to disregard the result. It is true that we, as teachers, are mostly interested in the language practice that takes place during the discussion itself; but the students are at least equally, if not more, interested in its apparent purpose, whose achievement is represented by the results of the task. What the groups have done must then be displayed and related to in some way by teacher and class: assessed, criticized, admired, argued with, or even simply listened to with interest. This I call the *feedback* session; it is an essential part of the activity as a whole and may provide a setting for some valuable learning.

Feedback can be organized in a multitude of different ways: by giving the 'correct' results, where there are any, and getting groups to assess their own success; by trying to collate the various proposals into a definitive class version; by comparing the conclusions of different groups; by simply asking groups to read aloud, display, or play back their results. It is particularly interesting for one group that has been working on a certain assignment to find out how the others have coped with it; I am always pleased to find how attentive students are when listening to descriptions of what other groups have made of the same material they have had.

In most cases a brief full class session is needed and some sort of rounding-off summary by the teacher. It is most important not to leave the problems set hanging in the air (unless it is planned to continue in a further session), to supply all the necessary solutions, to answer queries as far as possible, and to give students time and scope for exploring conflicts and differences that come out of comparing results. Sometimes the teacher may find it advisable to publish the results in some way: to pin them up on the board or type them out for distribution.

So much for the feedback on results, which may be done by teacher and class together; the feedback on process, however, is much more teacher-centred. The organization and performance of the debate sometimes need to be reacted to, assessed and criticized by the teacher, preferably immediately after the activity, if we are to take seriously the teaching of discussion skills. It is no good being indiscriminatingly warm and approving of students' work; they will appreciate being told exactly where and when their discussion could have been better, as well as where it was good. That this part of the lesson needs to be teacher-centred, incidentally, does not imply that it is teacher-monopolized; students' reactions and comments may also contribute to it.

Lastly, there is the feedback on the language use itself. Discussions provide the teacher with valuable information on what language is actively known and what is not, what is used rightly and what needs correction and practice. On the basis of this information she can then build further language lessons. These, of course, do not have to be immediately after the discussion; as far as the students are concerned there does not have to be any connection between the two, though the teacher may find it useful to point it out.

Conclusion

To summarize: discussions or discussion–games are the best vehicle for fluency practice in a foreign language: the question is how to make these maximally effective. *Interesting topics, group-work,* and *role-play* can facilitate student interaction. A *task* which cannot be done without verbal communication supplies learners with a reason to speak, and thus makes for a higher degree of naturalness and enthusiasm in their discourse. Finally, discussions can be made very much more efficient and enjoyable if attention is given to their *organization*.

It has been said that there is nothing so practical as a good theory; and I hope this may be true of the theoretical ideas of Part 1. Their application in practice forms the basis of Part 2, where a number of actual discussions that work are described in detail.

Part 2: Practical examples

Introduction

Nearly all the task-centred communication activities suggested in the second part of this book are based on exercises I have done myself with students. They may be used as they stand, or serve as bases for further original variations. In either case, I hope teachers will find them as effective as I have done.

As the aim of these discussions is fluency practice, it is in general assumed that the participants already know enough English to produce the structures and vocabulary necessary. Occasionally, however, where the activities are appropriate for more elementary levels, I have indicated some of the language items to be revised before beginning the discussion. Teachers who wish their students to practise certain structures can of course direct them accordingly before the talking begins. This alters the character of the activity somewhat: the emphasis moves from spontaneous fluent talk to specific grammar-practice, albeit communication-based. If, for example, participants in a guessing game are instructed beforehand to use a certain type of question rather than any other, then this question will probably be very effectively practised; but the game as a whole will have lost some of its value as an opportunity for free interaction in the foreign language.

Task-centred discussions are composed of one or both of two elements: the 'brainstorm' and the 'organization'. Broadly speaking, these represent the creative and analytic aspects respectively; 'brainstorming' is the technique whereby members of the group let loose a hail of possible solutions or suggestions, in random order as they occur to them; it can be followed by the processing of this material into an order and shape which will constitute the eventual answer(s) to the original problem ('organizing'). Sometimes the list of brainstormed ideas may be enough in itself (as in *Ideas from a central theme,* pp. 35–9); sometimes the raw material is given and all the group has to do is organize it (as in *Choosing candidates* (a), pp. 73–9). Sometimes the two processes may be merged into one another or follow one another. But in any case, I have found it convenient to divide the activities into three sections: *brainstorming, organizing,* and *compound.* They (the activities) are roughly in order of difficulty, with the simplest at the beginning and the most sophisticated towards the end.

Many of the ideas were borrowed or adapted from books or fellow-teachers. Where I remember and can identify the sources, I have mentioned them; but there are bound to be omissions, for which I apologize in advance. Many excellent books and periodicals give further advice and ideas; a selection of these is given in the *Bibliography*.

Each activity is described as follows: a general opening section gives its basic form and procedure, with notes on language input where relevant; specific variations are then described in detail, with examples of material that might be used. An exception to this is the first activity, *Guessing games,* whose different versions, though simple in themselves, are very varied and numerous; I have therefore described them under four headings: *Organization, Variations, Subjects* and *Language Input*.

Brainstorming activities

1 Guessing games

Guessing is one of the simplest and most well-known brainstorming activities that exist, and is very easily transformed into a group discussion game (using 'discussion' in the wide sense defined earlier). There are many variations, but in its essence, the guessing game is a process of discovery by one individual or group of an item of information known to another, with some limitation on its transmission (for instance, that the 'knower' may only say 'yes' or 'no'). There are always two sides, called here the 'knower(s)' and the 'guesser(s)'. Sometimes, in its crudest form, a game may just consist of a sequence of random guesses until the right answer is hit on. In more sophisticated versions, the field is gradually and systematically narrowed until the solution is inevitable. The guessing game lends itself to use by classes whose English is comparatively limited, since it is based on the simplest types of utterances: simple questions or statements, brief phrases, single words.

Organization

It is preferable, in a guessing game based on questions, that only one or two of the participants be knowers and the majority guessers, because nearly all the verbal activity in a game of this type is the asking. It is all too easy even for experienced teachers to overlook this point: where only one student guesses, all the others are limited to 'yes', 'no' or simple stereotyped agreements or disagreements, while the luckless guesser has to rack his brains for a sequence of questions and their correct formulation – with long gaps while he tries to think what to say next.

The guessing usually needs to be stimulated not only by the knowledge that there is something to be guessed, but also by some hint as to its nature: the first letter of its name, its colour, function, or material, or just any random hint at the discretion of the knower.

Another addition that may improve tension and enjoyment is the limiting of the number of questions or negative answers allowed (as in 'Twenty Questions'). However, this may in some cases lead to long pauses for preparation or formulation of maximally useful questions, in which case it is, for us, counterproductive. In general, such stipulations are more appropriate for adult or advanced classes.

As to the presentation and beginning of the game: if the majority are knowers, then the guesser is asked to close his eyes or absent himself for a short time while the subject is displayed or decided; if there is only one knower, then he may be given a piece of paper with the answer written or drawn on it. If the subjects are to be thought up by the students themselves, then it is a good idea to give the whole class a minute or two to think of subjects before the game begins: this saves gaps later, particularly if each successful guesser is to become the next knower.

It is usually advisable to have a 'trial run' with the whole class before dividing into groups.

Variations

One excellent variation on the guessing game is based not on questions but on statements. In this, most of the group are knowers, and only one a guesser. The latter does little actual guessing; the bulk of the work is done by the knowers who throw out hint after hint about the solution, in the form of simple positive or negative statements. The number of conjectures finally allowed to the guesser is limited to three, and made only when he is fairly sure he is right. If, for example, the group has thought of 'a horse', then hints might be: 'It's an animal', 'It has four legs', 'We don't have one in school', 'It doesn't usually live in water', 'Many people think it beautiful', and so on. This is really an exercise in finding things to say, more or less at random, on a subject, but supplied with a purpose by the presence of a guesser. Again, it can be played at all levels.

Guessing games can also take the form of group competitions. A pool of pieces of paper with suitable subjects written or drawn on them is placed at an accessible point in the classroom. One member from each group draws one piece of paper and returns with it to his group who have to guess its subject in the shortest possible time. When they have guessed it, they retain the paper, and another member goes to draw the next subject. If they fail, they return the paper to the pool. The winning group is the one with the most pieces of paper at the end.

Another variation can be played in fours, bridge-style, one couple versus another. A pool of pieces of paper bearing the names of the subjects to be guessed is placed face-down on the table. One participant picks a piece of paper at random and defines or describes its subject. If his partner can guess the correct answer, the couple wins that paper; if not, it is discarded or returned to the pool. It is now the turn of the other couple. The partners take it in turns to be guessers and knowers; and, again, the ones with the most pieces of paper at the end are the winners.

Another refinement which can be introduced into most guessing games is to forbid the knower to use the words 'yes' or 'no'. This forces more flexible and sophisticated use of the language, and adds further tension.

Subjects

It is sometimes not realized quite how wide is the range of subjects which can be used for guessing games. Things, animals, professions, celebrities are frequently used; but interesting guessing processes can be based also on actions or locations, and others on combinations of some or all of these subjects, and on undefined, mixed topics.

The most well-known guessing game is that based on the guessing of *things:* common objects, animals, sometimes even abstracts or events. These may be physically present or represented by a picture or the written word. The more adult the class, the less the need for physical representation of the subject.

Hints to focus thinking may be of various kinds. 'I Spy', for example, combines two hints: that the subject is visible to the knower, and that it begins with a certain letter ('I spy with my little eye something beginning with B'). In 'Animal–Vegetable–Mineral' the knower gives a broad definition of the material(s) from which the subject is made. Or the knower may think up his own hint in terms of size, colour, his attitude to it, or whatever he likes. He may then amplify this hint if the group has trouble guessing.

Finding suitable subjects for such games is sometimes a problem. If one does not wish to take advantage of the imagination of the students themselves, but to give arbitrary subjects they have no way of knowing, it is time-consuming and wearying trying to think up enough original and appropriate ideas. It is sometimes useful to think in terms of categories: I hope the list below may help.

Subjects for elementary students:
Classroom equipment: table, chair, pencil, pen . . .
Outdoors: tree, house, mountain, river . . .

Clothing: dress, shoes, shirt, trousers . . .
Parts of the body: head, foot, hand, ear, nose . . .
Food: bread, meat, apple, coffee, sugar . . .
Animals/Birds/Insects: dog, cat, mouse, fish . . .
Transport: car, aeroplane, bicycle, bus . . .
Implements: plate, knife, hammer, gun . . .

Subjects for intermediate and advanced students:
Classroom equipment: typewriter, light bulb, felt-tip pen,
   transparency . . .
Outdoors: cliff, estuary, lava, plateau . . .
Clothing: tights, clogs, earring, cloak . . .
Parts of the body: elbow, kidney, toenail, lung, jaw . . .
Food: roll, chop, marmalade, sauce . . .
Animals/Birds/Insects: cobra, hare, swallow, wasp, vulture . . .
Transport: hovercraft, bulldozer, skateboard, lift . . .
Implements: food mixer, razor, mallet, sub-machine gun . . .

More difficult; subjects are parts of items:
Classroom equipment: pencil-lead, book cover, nail in wall . . .
Outdoors: slope, tree trunk, roof, peak . . .
Clothing: button, buckle, thread, hem . . .
Parts of the body: muscle, vein, blood corpuscle, skin . . .
Food: peel, core, marrow, grain of flour, egg yolk . . .
Animals/Birds/Insects: snout, paw, tail, fur, wing, beak, shell,
   fin . . .
Transport: tyre, internal combustion engine, gauge . . .
Implements: handle, blade, plug, bullet . . .

More complex or comprehensive subjects, 'happenings': this lesson, the
rush-hour traffic, a meal, a zoo, London, a University, the Second
World War . . .

Abstracts or semi-abstracts: anger, sadness, beauty, advice, pleasure,
democracy, communism, authority, love, dancing,
agriculture . . .

Guessing *professions or celebrities* is also fun, especially when the
knower role-plays his subject. If it is a profession, the hint
can consist of a mime and/or the usual sex of its practitioner. If it
is an actual personality, then it is usually enough to give the sex.
   It would be of little value to give a suggested list of celebrities
for guessing, as such lists are too dependent on time and place.
A list appropriate to a class studying in Canada in 1980 would be
unsuitable for their contemporaries in India, and out of date
anyway by 1985. However, I append some suggested professions.

At the elementary level: policeman, actor, singer, doctor, nurse, engineer, teacher, housewife, farmer, secretary, manager, professor, shopkeeper, student, soldier, pilot, scientist, driver, gardener, factory worker, artist, baker, musician, cowboy, king, president, writer, builder, dressmaker, painter.

At the intermediate and advanced levels: agent, solicitor, civil engineer, chiropodist, cosmetician, foreman, bricklayer, fishmonger, social worker, radio operator, commando, frogman, caretaker, sculptor, cellist, shorthand-typist, receptionist, minister, bee-keeper, confectioner, interior designer, architect, dustman, photographer, mathematician, physicist, pianist, air-hostess.

Actions can also be guessed. In the simplest version of this, the knower mimes something, which may be as straightforward as reading a newspaper, or as complicated as carrying out repairs on a car. Or he may imagine doing it or having done it: the questions may thus be in the past or the present. I have a packet of pictures cut out of magazines, which are very useful for this game. Each picture depicts some sort of activity. The knower takes a card, gives a hint as to the subject performing the action ('a woman', 'a dog', 'two boys') and lets the others guess.

As for examples, one finds oneself depending on stereotypes such as 'reading books', 'drinking', 'opening the door' etc. It is useful to have a ready-made list available, whether in the form of pictures, as described above, or as written notes. On the whole, elementary actions are based on general daily activities, whereas advanced ones are very specific, or dependent on individual professions.

At the elementary level: reading, writing, opening books or doors, eating, drinking, dancing, riding, watching television, walking, running, sleeping, waking up, brushing teeth, dressing, playing games, talking, cleaning.

At the intermediate and advanced levels: cooking or eating specific foods, repairing apparatus, buying or selling something, solving a particular problem, watching a known programme on television, cleaning a specific object, travelling by a specific means of transport, meeting/leaving different kinds of people, arresting a criminal, giving some medical treatment to a patient, doing an experiment, making a commercial transaction of some kind.

Guessing *locations* in answer to an imaginative question such as 'Where is the gold hidden?' can also be entertaining and suitable for quite young or elementary classes, particularly if the possible places are limited to the immediate environment. For more advanced classes, the imagination can have free play, and the gold (or whatever) can be hidden as far away as outer space, Antarctica, the thirty-first storey of the Empire State Building, or wherever you like. The game can be made more interesting by basing it on an imagined dramatic situation. For example, the teacher could introduce it like this: 'The time-mechanism of an atom-bomb is ticking away, and can only be stopped by pressing the button of a small transmitter. The only one who knows where the transmitter is, is this robot' (the knower), 'who, however, cannot speak, but can only answer yes or no. You have exactly three minutes to find out where it is.' Both young and mature learners enjoy the simulated tension.

No list of suggested location-subjects is given, since these are too dependent on the location of the class itself and the background of the students.

Finally, the subject of a guessing game can be a combination of two or more elements out of those described above; for example, the solution may consist of 'I am watching television in my room' or 'the President of the U.S.A. is signing letters in Camp David'. Such subjects take much longer to guess, but the process is encouraged by partial successes along the way as each element is discovered. The teacher may insist on the exact original sentence being discovered, or be content with a reasonably accurate paraphrase. This variation is suitable for adult or advanced classes.

Language input

At the most basic level, questions are asked simply in the form of a guess at the answer with a rising inflection: *A horse? A cup? A policeman?* Next, there are all forms of 'yes–no' questions; if an object or animal is to be guessed, the participants will use forms such as: *Is it big? Does it live in Africa? Can we eat it?* Slightly more complex, but still at the elementary level, when guessing at people, professions, plural subjects, historical figures, we can vary the above in number, person and tense: *Are they in the classroom? Do you meet people in your work? Did she live in the nineteenth century?* For guessing at actions, questions in the present progressive are usually appropriate, but the past can also be used: *Are you making something? Did you dance/ Were you dancing?* and for guessing locations, prepositional phrases, with or without the preliminary interrogative form: *(Is it) in this building? (Are you) outside this country?* At a more sophisticated level, much more subtle tenses can be employed (though students may need specific instructions or encouragement to use them!): *Would I have been likely to meet her at court? Could I be treated by you?*

This type of game is particularly useful for teachers whose students do not, in their native language, invert the verb and its subject to form questions, and therefore have trouble producing correct interrogative forms in English. On the other hand, it is worth noting at this point that native speakers playing such games often skip the formal question structure altogether and more naturally ask: *A poet? Playing tennis? In London?* or use declarative questions such as: *It's a rabbit? You do this often?* and if we are interested chiefly in fluency, these forms should be acceptable.

As to the statement-based game described on p. 28, the range of language forms is as wide or narrow as the students' imagination and knowledge will take them. At the elementary level one would want perhaps to make sure that participants have mastered the use of *is* and *are* (non-existent in a number of languages, for example, Arabic), and the basic tenses, in particular the present simple.

2 Finding connections

The thinking basis here is the search for common denominators or links between different items. Unlike guessing games, these activities are unsuitable for the very earliest stages of language-learning; they can be used only with students who have a wide enough vocabulary to cope with the very extensive imaginative invention required, and who have a reasonable mastery of the tense system.

Connecting pairs

The group is given two elements – objects, people, abstract concepts, or combinations of these – and asked to find as many connections between them as possible, however tortuous. They might be asked to link a shoelace and an egg, or the President of the U.S.A. and a member of the class, or a helicopter and a drawing pin, a cigarette and nationalization or the number 24 and the colour purple. A connection between the first pair, for example, could simply be that the shoelace belongs to a man who likes eggs for breakfast; or that it came undone causing its owner to fall headlong into a market stall of eggs, or that the shoelace can be used to tie up a package of eggs.

The elements may be presented to the students in written form on slips of paper, or orally. Pictures are sometimes even better: a few minutes spent leafing through an old colour magazine with a pair of scissors handy will suffice for the preparation of a dozen recognizable and stimulating items; then it is up to the teacher to decide which to put with which. If you wish to use magazine pictures in this way, it is best to have no advance list of the concepts you are looking for – it takes far too long to find exactly what you want; better to use what the magazines happen to offer.

It is a good idea to give a different pair of items to each group, with a time-limit to think of all the connections that they can; and then to change over, repeating this several times until each group has worked on each combination. In the feedback, groups recount the resulting ideas to each other, which may be entertaining enough without further comment; zest may be added by awarding points to groups who have the most connections, or the most original ideas. Here are some further examples of pairs to be connected:

- an elephant and nail varnish
- a wedding and an ant
- a snowflake and a coin
- religious fanatics and a matchbox
- the number 25 and a master-criminal
- a (named) singer and a ladybird
- a silkworm and an axe
- love and a rubbish dump
- a pen and a new-born baby
- the Garden of Eden and a bar of soap

Combining elements into a story

The group is given three or more incongruous elements like those suggested above and asked to make up a story or coherent passage of prose which includes them all. These elements may be presented all together and given to the group as a whole, or one may be given to each participant to work into the story as his turn comes (see p. 15). Usually words are used, but, as in the previous exercise, sets of cut-out magazine pictures may serve as well or better. The advantage of pictures is that they can include far more detail and action than simple words: their disadvantage is that they cannot depict abstracts.

The process may be lengthened or made more entertaining by the addition of an extra word or picture just when the group thinks it has completed the task. The results should be written down or recorded so that they may be presented to the rest of the class in the feedback session. If feasible, all groups should work on the same set of stimuli: this makes the different results much more entertaining. Examples are given in more or less ascending level of difficulty.

- paper, afraid, foot, slow, seventy-five, quickly.
- lion, telephone, happily, green, dance, milk.
- the President, river, key, apple, smile, angrily, how are you?
- actor, grandfather, eye, snake, move, go away, hard.
- electric, ski, oily, dramatically, Robin Hood, hippopotamus.
- squeeze, crocodile, explosion, vegetarian, pure, violin.
- shoot, ventriloquist, potato, guilty, slippery, anxious.
- jungle, telephone, bride, renew, microbe, religiously.
- egg-shaped, model, atmosphere, lawfully, caricature, congratulate.
- fossil, suburb, incoherent, whip, obstruction, polygamous.

Finding things in common

The class is divided into pairs, and partners are asked to find as many things in common with each other as they can. This, incidentally, is an excellent ice-breaking exercise for a class whose members are not yet acquainted, as it entails finding out about one another and seeking points of contact. Doing the same in threes may be a later elaboration; this is more difficult and means much more thorough research into each other's backgrounds, tastes, characters, etc.

This exercise should be done fairly briskly, and should not go on very long. Afterwards, detailed recounting of all the points of contact found may become rather overlong and boring; it is better for couples to state simply how many points they found. Alternatively, the teacher may ask for any particularly original or surprising ideas.

3 Ideas from a central theme

This in a way is the converse of the process of finding connections. Instead of the students being given elements and looking for a common base, the base is given and related elements sought. The language needed may be very simple, hence some variations of this exercise are suitable for elementary levels.

The main structures needed here are modals expressing possibility or suggestion, in phrases such as: *You can/could use . . . , We may need . . . , We might have . . . , Could we include . . . ? I should like to . . . , Might I suggest . . . ? Could you really . . . ? Why might you . . . ?*

Qualities

The group is given an abstract quality of colour, shape, texture, structure, nature, function or activity, and asked to think of as many things as it can that possess it. Brownness, for example, roundness or (more difficult) spirality, roughness or mucosity. The very fact that most of these words are usually adjectives and form more or less awkward abstract nouns indicates that the abstract idea is an unusual one; it is interesting and stimulating to focus thinking from this angle. For the same reason, however, it is simpler to present the subject to classes in the more usual adjectival form, or in phrases such as 'things that are red'. A trial run with the whole class is advisable, in order to open their minds to the possibilities: then groups can be set separate or parallel subjects. Here are some examples (again in ascending order of difficulty):

- things that are red/yellow/green/black
- things that are round/square/flat/oval/spiral
- things that go in twos/threes/groups
- things that are soft/hard/liquid
- things that can fly/float/jump
- things that have holes in
- things worked by electricity/muscle/oil
- things made of plastic/metal/wood/glass
- symmetrical things
- things that move fast/slowly/in curves
- things that give pleasure

Associations

Associations, like *Qualities,* can be a very easy game, because in its simplest form it requires only single words or the simplest expressions. Here also a central theme is given, but in this case the group is asked to list concepts that are merely associated with it in some way, without actually possessing any particular quality themselves. This exercise is therefore more wide-ranging than the previous one and can go on longer; suggestions do not have to be limited to nouns. Here, for example, is a list of associations a group might get out of 'paper': writing, ink, pen, pencil, book, inflammable, document, typewriter, cardboard, thin, white, coloured, cut-up, publish, lined, squared, tissue, parchment, communication, letters, read, journalist, stenography, decipher, advertise. Less obvious items have to be justified by their proposers: chains (you make chains from coloured paper for decoration), boats (you can make paper boats for children), cracks (as in the phrase 'paper over the cracks').

If each group gets the same theme, then the activity can be competitive; the winning group has the most associations – and can justify them all! But reading out complete lists of items can be boring: one interesting way of varying feedback (when groups have been given different themes) is for one member of the group to begin reading the list and see how quickly other groups can identify the theme.

Subjects for *Associations* should be more concrete and specific than those for *Qualities,* but not too much so: 'wheel', for example, is a good subject, whereas 'roundness' is too general, and 'tyre' too limiting. Here are some possible themes:

> money, religion, water, travel, family, ground, seeing, hearing, thinking, city, bottle, medicine, theatre, fire, cold.

Uses of an object

Each group is supplied with an object and told to list as many imaginative uses for it as they can think of. All groups may have the same object, or each may be different; in the latter case, objects may be 'rotated' during the course of the session. In any case it is a good idea for each group by the end to have worked on the same object(s) as the others, so that results can be compared.

This is a particularly entertaining exercise, and is good as a competition, each group trying to outdo the others in the number, variety and originality of its suggestions. I once gave an adult group a toothbrush to do this exercise with; and apart from obvious uses such as brushing your teeth or cleaning typewriters, they also came up with ideas like back-scratching, straightening eyebrows, playing the drum, and so on. Any such use is acceptable, provided it is physically feasible!

All this can be done, of course, in the absence of any actual object, but it is usually more effective if it is physically present, to be looked at and handled. To find a few small household objects and bring them to the classroom should not be difficult; and this is all the preparation that is necessary. Here are some possible objects:

> toothbrush, hat, umbrella, knife, pencil, cup, match, pillow-case, bottle, blob of plasticine, tweezers, scarf, coin, toilet roll, ruler.

What will you need?

This is a less amusing but more practical exercise along the same lines. The group is told it is facing some sort of fairly elaborate operation and has to make a list of the equipment needed and/or jobs to be done. One can start from something relatively simple like making a cake, progress to a more complex project like preparing a hiking trip, and go on, if one is really ambitious, to set up house or equip a school (see *Planning projects,* pp. 112–8 for a more advanced version of this).

There is plenty of scope for role-play here. In the school-equipping activity, for example, the group could be a committee considering the refurnishing of a school damaged by fire. This committee could consist of some or all of the following characters: the principal, a pupils' representative, the librarian, the head of the science department, the head of the humanities department, the sports teacher, a parent – with or without defined personalities and attitudes.

Groups may be required to copy their lists on to the blackboard or acetate film for the overhead projector so that they can be displayed and compared. As a later addition, the teacher may introduce the factor of a limited budget for the project, so that proposals will need to be fined down to essentials or priorities, and a definitive class list evolved on this basis. Here are some examples:

– Making a cake/stew/curry/meal
– Preparing a day by the sea/picnic
– Preparing a hiking/cycling/camping trip
– Preparing an outfit for a new baby/bride/student going away to study
– Furnishing an office/school/bed-sitting room
– Giving a party/wedding

Characteristics

What are the characteristics of a good teacher? A ruler? A mother? Each group collects ideas from all participants and forms a list. Some refinements of this: the group may later be required to put the characteristics in order of priority (see *Features and functions,* p. 72), cut them down to the ten most important ones, or expand them to describe exhaustively the most perfect teacher, ruler, mother, etc. Here are some examples of possible subjects:

friend, wife/husband*, baby*, doctor, actor, mother, company director, mother-in-law★, athlete, detective, soldier★, secretary, landlady, teacher★, ruler★.

Possible characteristics of those subjects marked with an asterisk can be found at the end of *Features and functions*, (p. 72).

4 Implications and interpretations

This category, as its name implies, is open to enormous variation. It is really a slightly more sophisticated version of *Ideas from a central theme*. It consists of exploring the implications and interpretations of a more or less ambiguous stimulus, which may take the form of an imaginary situation, a picture, a noise, or a doodle. The language may be relatively simple, but it is not limited to specific structures or vocabulary.

Doodles

In Fig. 1 there are examples of various doodles which were drawn as abstracts, but which may be interpreted as having specific meanings. The first, for example, could be a road map, or bits of apple peel thrown on the floor, or an ancient hieroglyphic, or minute organisms seen under the microscope. The group is required to think up a certain number of interpretations, or as

Fig. 1

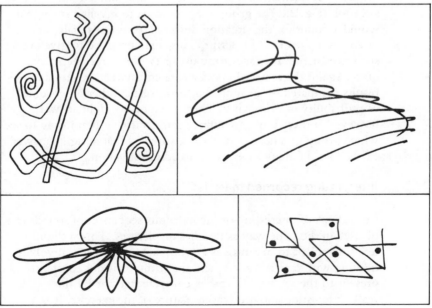

many as it can, or as many as it can in a certain time. Every
member of the group should contribute at least one suggestion.
When one doodle's possibilities have been exhausted, the
group moves on to the next, taken from a pool in an easily
available position in the classroom. The group secretary may note
down the best suggestions, to be compared later with those of
the other groups. One would have to decide beforehand what one
means by 'best' in this context: most likely? most unlikely? most
original? most amusing?

It is possible to play this without previously prepared doodles.
One student scribbles a design on the blackboard, overhead
projector, or other easily visible surface, and invites the others to
hazard interpretations; he then selects the best contribution, and
the student who made it draws the next doodle. This is a brisk
ongoing activity which may be done in the full class forum,
provided there are not too many students.

Interpreting pictures

Putting meaning into meaningless doodles is one possibility; but
another is to take pictures which already have some meaning –
albeit ambiguous – and to find different, deeper, more subtle or
detailed interpretations. Photographs or paintings culled from
colour magazines are a rich source of such material; or the teacher
may be talented enough to make her own. The only necessity is
the clear representation of a more or less dramatic but unexplained
situation (Fig. 2). The group may be asked to invent a story that
would account for the situation depicted, or write a dialogue,
or an extract from a film script. They may be asked to give one
such explanation for each stimulus, or two or three alternative
ones. Again, the material may be rotated between groups and the
results compared to, or judged against, one another on grounds
of probability or originality. There need be no 'right answer';
however, if there is one (genuine or arbitrary), it is amusing to see
which group gets nearest; and the awareness that a 'right' answer
exists does, in many cases, seem to add motivation.

Interpreting recorded material

Recordings of interesting or incongruous sequences of sounds can
be used in the same way as doodles or pictures. This is slightly
less convenient to organize as a group activity, since it involves
fiddling with tape recorders, and the stimulus is not constantly
present to the senses; but that is compensated for by the
really interesting and motivating nature of the exercise. It is

Fig. 2a

Fig. 2b

Fig. 2c

Fig. 2d

possible, but tricky and time-consuming to compose one's own tapes; however there are two ready-made recordings of such noise-sequences available (see *Bibliography*).

Since noises are fleeting and, when not immediately recognizable, difficult to recall, some warming-up activities may be advisable to familiarize the students with the material. After a first hearing, each group tries to recall and list the sequence of sounds, identifying them where possible. After hearing the tape a second time, they correct their list, and describe the noises in more detail. After the third time, they are on their own – to make up stories or action-sequences that will account for the sounds. Later the results can be read out or described while the tape is running, using the original noises as background sound-effects.

Short unexplained dialogues may be used in the same way as sound-sequences. Here, the warming-up session is less essential, and one or two hearings, without recall exercises, may suffice. The interpretation in this case includes not only situation and action, but also characters and relationships. Indeed, the teacher may limit the interpretation to only one of these: 'What do you think is the relationship between the two speakers?' 'What do you think is the character of the first speaker? The second?' and so on. In the absence of a tape-recorder, incidentally, the same exercise can easily be carried out using written material: most published tapes of recorded dialogues are accompanied by written transcripts (see *Bibliography*). In this case the stimulus is certainly less vivid, but on the other hand it is far more open to varying interpretations: there is no hint as to the sex or mood of the speakers, nor any emphasis, pauses or intonation; all this can be supplied by the students.

Character studies

Character studies can also be based on magazine pictures, drawings or, as in my examples, on clear photographs which can be easily reproduced (Fig. 3). The group is given a portrait and asked to make up a complete description of the person depicted. If this is felt to be too vague, the task may be more clearly defined by first of all requiring the group to make a list of things they might want to find out about a stranger. Such a list might include, for example, name, age, education, family background, profession, income, likes, dislikes, interests, ambitions, problems. Armed with this list, the students will find it easier to discuss the character of the person. Again, rotating pictures between groups makes the comparing of results more fun.

Fig. 3a

Fig. 3b

Fig. 3c

Fig. 3d

Men from Mars

One can also approach well-known objects as if they were unknown and try to define them. This stretches the imagination somewhat, and is an amusing exercise. The group is told that it is composed of members of an extra-terrestrial civilization who for the first time are coming into contact with certain terrestrial artefacts, such as a toothbrush, a watch, a pencil sharpener. Without reference to human civilization, about which they know nothing, the participants have to find out (and, optionally, write down) everything they possibly can about the object from its mere presence, and then try to draw plausible conclusions as to its function. The objects listed at the end of *Uses of an object* (p. 37) are suitable for this exercise too. Here are some further possibilities:

> pencil-sharpener, watch, needle, paintbrush, ring, paper, ashtray, glove, light bulb, button, key, reel of thread.

Foreseeing results

Can you think of all the implications of an event such as the outbreak of civil war in your country? the discovery of huge resources of oil in your area? everyone suddenly going colour-blind? The group sets itself to brainstorming all the possible results of such eventualities. They may do this as a straight-forward discussion, or through role-playing various characters, each of whom is interested in the effects on his or her own life or sphere of activity: a mother, the ruler of the country, a doctor, a child. Or the roles could be rather those of attitude: the optimist, the pessimist, the coward, the money-grabber, the power-seeker, the philanthropist. As a follow-up after the results have been displayed and discussed, the groups may be asked to try to decide what measures should be taken to anticipate or cope with those implications which appear problematical.

Some suggestions for subjects for this exercise are listed below. All begin with 'What would happen if . . .'

– civil war broke out?
– vast resources of oil were discovered here?
– everyone went colour-blind?
– everyone forgot how to read?
– the wind stopped?
– there were no clouds?
– we were all telepathic?

– stretches of water more than a kilometre wide could not be crossed?
– tobacco and alcohol were made illegal?
– all drugs were legal and cheaply available?

Explanations

This in a way is the opposite of *Foreseeing results*. Instead of giving a cause and asking students to imagine the results, we give them results and ask them to reconstruct the cause(s). Groups are given a description of an apparently incredible or incongruous set of circumstances; the more details there are, the longer and more interesting the discussion will be. The classic example of such a situation is the famous *Marie Celeste* mystery: a ship found floating on the ocean without crew or passengers, no sign of violence, and everything in good working order; but obviously hastily abandoned, with meals half-eaten and jobs half-done. The group has to think up a logical (if far-fetched) explanation that fits all the facts; a kind of exercise in detection.

Good, imaginative groups can do this quite quickly, so, if you have such students, it is best to base the discussion on several different situations which can rotate between groups. However, others may have difficulty in getting going; sometimes a group faced with a complex situation of this kind just does not know where to begin, and the result is long puzzled silences. Giving the facts gradually may help to ease them in: they can be given at first only the basic situation in the form of the first few words of the description. After a few minutes they can be presented with further information which may mean revising their original explanation. After a further time–lapse they can be given another detail, and so on, until they have it all. This makes the organization of the discussion simpler (for the students, anyway!), and the process of hypothesis-testing more systematic.

If role-play is used, then the group becomes a team of professional investigators called in to solve the enigma. Information can then be provided in the form of 'telephone messages' or notes in sealed envelopes, and 'witnesses' can be interviewed. Further evidence can be improvised and presented during the discussion, provided it does not contradict anything already known.

In the feedback, it is enough merely to have the groups report their explanations; the ingenuity and originality of these will be sufficiently interesting in themselves without further discussion or evaluation.

Below are some examples of the kind of thing I mean, in order of difficulty. Teachers may wish to make up their own; if so, I suggest detective fiction as a good source of inspiration, particularly the short stories of Agatha Christie, Conan Doyle and G.K. Chesterton.

a) A parcel was delivered to the school, addressed to a Mr Wilbur Welkins. Nobody had ever heard of him. The parcel was left on the staff-room table, and disappeared during the night.

b) A small boy, naked and with his head shaved, ran down a big city street. He was laughing happily though it was a cold day, and he had a photograph in his hand.

c) Footprints were discovered in the snow leading to a deserted Alpine hut. There were no footprints leaving, but the hut was empty except for a St Bernard dog and some books.

d) One of the school classrooms was found to be locked. The sound of a man groaning was heard from within. When it was broken into, it was discovered that most of the furniture had been smashed. There were two dead mice near the door and a strong smell of burnt rubber in the air.

e) Mrs Smith, a housewife, affectionate wife, and mother of two small children, was digging in her garden the other day when she found a small metal box in the earth. She called her neighbour, Mrs Jones, over to have a look; Mrs Jones went back into her house for a minute and then came out again. She found Mrs Smith staring at the open box with an expression of terror on her face. The box was hot to the touch and there was nothing in it but some blue dust. Mrs Smith was taken to the hospital where she fell into a deep sleep. On awakening she remembered nothing. Mrs Jones took the box to the police station where it was locked in the safe; but the next day it had disappeared.

f) The invading army arrived at a small village to find that all the villagers seemed to be dead. There was no sign of violence; the people were lying in neat rows in the village square with strange smiles on their faces. On some of the bodies were traces of a green liquid. Eventually a child was found who was still alive; he had no tongue and could not speak, but in answer to questions he pointed at the sky and then drew a mark in the sand in the shape of a V. The commander of the army did not know what to think, but, influenced by the superstitious terror of his soldiers, withdrew without touching anything. He did not report the incident, but the story spread and no-one has been near the village since.

Organizing activities

5 Comparing

These exercises are based on contrast and analogy: that is to say, they require students to discuss and define differences and similarities between various elements in order to carry out a task of classification.

As regards language input, advanced students need no preparation for these activities; elementary ones should be familiar at least with the following expressions: *both/neither/all, something/nothing in common, similar to/the same as/different from, odd man out, It doesn't fit because . . . , It is the only one that . . . , All the others . . . , the same kind (of thing) as . . . , the only one (that) . . . , That is/sounds/looks like . . . , That is/sounds/looks different from . . . They are alike/different because . . .*

Odd man out

The process of selecting an odd man out from a given set of items will probably be familiar to teachers; it provides the basis for a fairly popular vocabulary exercise. However, it is not usually exploited for discussion purposes. This is partly because it does not spontaneously generate conversation (like the story-telling activity described on p. 15, it would seem to be more naturally done silently as individual work), and partly because, even if students do solve it by talking, the over-simple and convergent nature of the task does not allow for much negotiation. However, some simple tactics of presentation and process can overcome these objections and transform the exercise into a stimulating discussion.

Firstly, as in exercises previously described, the complete set of items does not have to be given to the group as a whole; each student can be given only one or two, so that a contribution from each is necessary for the finished result. Secondly, these sets do not need to be made up in the usual way with several similar items and one obviously different. We are not here testing our students' knowledge of vocabulary, or I.Q., we simply want them to talk; hence it is much better for our purposes to have lists with *no* obvious odd man out so that a fair amount of deliberation

is needed in order to decide which one to select. Or we can
vary and extend the task by requiring the group to find some
justification for selecting *each* item as the odd one, or by asking
each participant to justify his own.

Let us take, for example, a simple set of items: horse, cat,
mouse, camel, lion, cow. Each may be considered the odd one
out:

> horse: the only one commonly used for sport
> cat: the only one which drinks milk
> mouse: the only pest
> camel: the only one which lives in the desert
> lion: the only one which may eat man
> cow: the only one commonly occurring in large groups

Of course, these are not completely foolproof distinctions – some
may be arguably inaccurate – but that does not matter; in fact it
may be all to the good, in that it supplies further basis for
argument and therefore talk. Further sets of items for this activity:

– apple, orange, mango, banana, grape, peach.
– India, China, France, Uganda, U.S.A., New Guinea.
– finger, blood, heart, eye, muscle, tongue.
– sock, coat, dress, underpants, scarf, jeans.
– Red Riding Hood, Hansel and Gretel, Snow White, Sleeping
  Beauty, Goldilocks, Cinderella.
– tree, bush, flower, weed, plant, grass.
– trumpet, drum, violin, flute, harp, piano.
– river, waterfall, lake, sea, marsh, puddle.
– quiet, angry, graceful, shy, modest, quick.
– peace, joy, harmony, beauty, delicacy, grace.

Categories

Perhaps the most usual application of the process of comparison is
sorting into categories. We do this all the time: dividing students
into different ability groupings in school, or sorting out larger and
smaller potatoes for cooking purposes are two examples. It will
easily be seen that the latter instance would be useless as a basis for
group discussion, whereas the former might be quite good,
because its solution is usually far from obvious, and it lends itself
to consultation. The problems in constructing a task of this
type are, in short, not unlike those described in *Odd man out;* and
their solutions are also similar.

One tactic is to compile sets of items in such a way that it is not
always clear to which category some elements may belong

(dividing students into ability groupings is a classic example of this, as many teachers know!). Another is to give extremely varied lists of items and let the group itself decide how to classify them. In this case, many different criteria can sometimes be found, and the lists can be divided and redivided three or more times, along different lines. It should also be made clear to the groups that they are not limited to two categories each time: they may divide items into three or even four. Let us take for example a list such as man, dog, baby, eagle, butterfly, lion, woman, hen, ant. The first time, the group may divide the items into human and non-human; the second, into beings that have two, four or six legs; the third into male, female or of undetermined sex; the fourth, into animals, birds and insects.

It may be found perfectly satisfactory to present the whole group with the full list (preferably duplicated, so that each participant may have his own); alternatively, each member can be given only part; or members can have 'overlapping' lists; that is to say, if there are twenty items in the full list, each member of a group of five might have a different random set of ten, which they can then try to categorize individually or in pairs before comparing notes in the full group discussion. This may turn out controversial, and the group might have to settle for decision by majority vote rather than unanimous agreement; but the latter should be aimed for, and the vote used only as a last resort.

Since there has to be such a relatively large number of items, it is usually most practical to present them in the form of written lists. However, teachers with initiative (and time!) may wish to try using sets of small pictures or even bags of objects. As in most of these activities, the material may be rotated between groups and results compared.

In the example lists given below, the first three have set criteria, but the classification of some of the items is dubious and will vary from group to group. The next three each have three different sets of criteria, allowing for three divisions: these (criteria) may be given to the groups in advance, or they may be asked to find them out for themselves. In the last three examples, the group has to find its own criteria and then classify the items accordingly, in two or more different ways.

– To be divided into *essential/useful/not very useful:* pencil, feather, paper, hat, typewriter, picture, plate, thread, stone, knife, fork, bookmark, ashtray, rubber, sponge, toothpaste, cushion, safety-pin, towel.

– To be divided according to whether the students think they are *positive/negative* (or *good/bad*): nationalist, religious, imperialist, humanist, rightist, leftist, socialist, radical, liberal, feminist, racist, conservative, anarchist, fascist, democratic, segregationist, pacifist, idealist, militant, revolutionary, partisan, dissident.

– To be divided into *active/non-active:* sit, walk, run, block, oppose, die, love, try, fail, suit, hold, keep, have, suppose, appear, melt, lie, incline, collapse, compose, unite, agree, feel.

– To be divided into *man-made/natural, coloured/black/white/ transparent, edible/inedible/poisonous:* stone, air, paper, sea-water, baking-powder, glass, cake, whipped cream, coal, heroin, caviar, plastic, salt, worms, grass.

– To be divided into *human/non-human, physical/mental, desirable/undesirable* attributes: ugly, wooden, soft, hard, affectionate, egg-shaped, frightened, long, pretty, hollow, liquid, relaxed, useful, sexy, boastful, six-legged.

– To be divided into *big/small, animate/inanimate, singular/plural:* mouse, button, spiders, penknife, cow, house, elephants, mountains, diamond, body, flock, money, tower, paper, swarm of bees.

– To be divided *as the group decides:* Picasso, Joan of Arc, Jane Austen, Julius Caesar, Jackie Kennedy-Onassis, Shakespeare, de Gaulle, Marilyn Monroe, Florence Nightingale, Tito, Chekhov, Lenin, Newton, Moses, Eva Peron, Lawrence Olivier, Marie Curie, Cleopatra, D.H. Lawrence, Charlie Chaplin.

– To be divided *as the group decides:* London, Tokyo, Marseilles, Penang, New York, Los Angeles, Geneva, Brasilia, Sydney, Paris, Leningrad, Buenos Aires, Stockholm, Kabul, Glasgow, Calcutta, Alexandria, Johannesburg, Entebbe, Jerusalem, Ankara.

– To be divided *as the group decides:* well-dressed, gap-toothed, slim, chubby, broad-sholdered, tearful, muscular, bearded, little, grey-haired, lisping, tall, long-haired, barefoot, soprano.

6 Detecting differences

Again based on contrast and analogy, these exercises are, however, slightly different from those just described. The material does not consist of a collection of simple discrete items, but of compound, sometimes complicated, stimuli: pictures, descriptions, stories. Two, or possibly three, such stimuli are given to the students in such a way that they may not observe all of them simultaneously: they have to detect differences by remembering what has been said before or by comparing someone else's version with their own. Two such exercises are described: *Picture differences* and *Alibi*. Both are well-known, one as a puzzle, the other as a party-game; as language exercises, however, they need careful presentation and organization.

Notes on language input have been inserted into the description of each activity, rather than in a general introductory section; this is because the structures needed in each are quite different, in spite of the fact that the thinking processes are similar.

Picture differences

This will be familiar as a puzzle to most readers, and needs little adaptation to make it into a first-rate discussion activity. Pairs of pictures are prepared, identical except for a given number of small differences. Students are divided into pairs, each of whom gets a different version, and they have to discover the differences through speech alone; they are not allowed to see each other's pictures.

The complexity of this exercise can vary tremendously: simple pictures with a number of clear differences (see the *Park scene* in Fig. 4), involving elementary vocabulary, can be used even for beginner classes. For more advanced students, less easily described pictures and more subtle differences will be required. The difficulty does not necessarily increase with the number of differences to be detected; a well-motivated class will find it a challenge to try to cope with pairs of pictures that differ in only one or two respects. However, for classes who can do with constant encouragement, it is advisable to prepare pictures with ten to fifteen differences; every 'discovery' gives extra impetus to the interaction. Participants should be told how many differences there are, so that the task is clear, and they are continually aware of how well they are doing.

The preparation of such pictures is fairly simple and fun to do. You need a black and white line drawing (not photograph) with a fair amount of detail but without shades of grey (these do not reproduce well). The content of the drawing should not entail vocabulary beyond the level of the students. You photocopy it and then make the requisite number of alterations to the original drawing, using either a black fibre-tip pen (for additions) or white type-correcting fluid (for erasures). You then photocopy the altered version. The pairs of pictures can then be reproduced either on stencils or by further photocopying. My illustrations (Fig. 4) were made this way.

Fig. 4b

Fig. 4c

Two items of practical advice. Firstly, note down the alterations as you make them; it may be time-consuming and irritating trying to identify them later! Secondly, students tend to mark the differences they have identified on the actual pictures, by ringing them or marking them with an 'x'; to save having to reproduce new pictures every time you want to do the activity, it is wise to forbid this in advance, and make students write down their discoveries on separate pieces of paper; usually one-word notes will suffice.

An alternative is to use advertisements from magazines or newspapers: either two different advertisements for similar products, or one more or less symmetrical one cut down the middle. The number of differences here is much larger, of course, so students should be asked to find up to, say, seven differences in order to succeed.

The language needed here depends mostly on what is depicted; however, certain prepositions and expressions of place are essential in order to describe the positioning of different components of a picture.

Prepositions: *in, on, under, behind, in front of, between, among, over, under, above, through, beside, next to, to the left/right of.*

Expressions of place: *at the bottom/top, on the left/right, in the middle, at the edge, in the foreground/background, in the top/bottom/ left-hand/right-hand corner.*

Sentences will mostly be in the form of simple declarative descriptions; for example: *The man's nose is long and he has a stick. There are two trees behind the castle.* But questions will also naturally be used, as: *Is your policeman fat? How many trees do you have in your picture? Are there apples in your tree? Is there anything behind the wall?* Or combinations of questions and statements, as: *I have six dogs in my picture; how many do you have? The two women are both wearing dresses, aren't they?*

Solutions to the pairs of pictures shown in Fig. 4 are given below; they are expressed in terms of the changes made to the bottom picture in each case.

a) *Shakespeare cartoon*
1) Shakespeare's eyes are down.
2) There is no pen in the ink-bottle on the table.
3) There is no crumpled paper by Shakespeare's foot.
4) Shakespeare has a hole in his shoe.
5) There are two rows of nails in the side of the table.
6) Shakespeare has only one eyebrow.
7) There is no comma after the first 'to be'.
8) There are only two dots after the word 'catchy'.

b) *Railway station*
1) There is no piece of paper on the floor.
2) The woman has five buttons on her coat.
3) There is no arrow by the word 'Buffet' on the notice.
4) The woman has no earring.
5) The little boy has black stripes on his jersey.
6) There is no label attached to the suitcase handle.
7) There is a sticker on the suitcase saying 'London'.
8) There is no hour-hand on the clock.
9) The man in the window has a black cup.
10) There is no 'Buffet' notice on the window.
11) The man inside the buffet with his back to us has long hair.
12) There is no boy's face in the poster on the extreme right.

c) *Office scene*
1) There is no hole in the back window.
2) There is no mousehole at the base of the back wall.
3) There is no eye in the clock-bird's head.
4) The flex of the electric kettle is black.
5) There is a switch at the side of the electric fire.
6) The time on the clock is seven o'clock.
7) There is no peeling wallpaper over the desk.
8) The stripe on the telephone-dial is black.
9) The coffee spilling from the cup at the right is black.
10) There is no keyhole in the door.
11) There is a pencil on the chair.
12) The typewriter-paper has writing on it.

d) *Park scene*
1) There is a band round the boy's hat.
2) The dark woman has shoelaces in both shoes.
3) The dark woman has three buttons down her front.
4) The fair woman has a necklace.
5) The bird on the dark woman's lap has two feet.
6) The horse of the statue has no eye.
7) The man of the statue has no hat.
8) There is a ball on the path behind the fair woman.
9) There is no gap in the buildings behind the statue.
10) There is a chimney to the right of the tree on the left.
11) There is writing on the stand under the statue.
12) There are birds in the sky.

Alibi

Two students are sent out of the room and told that they are
suspected of committing a crime between certain hours (for

example, that they robbed a well-known bank between the hours of ten and twelve last Thursday morning). They have to construct alibis for one another, claiming to have been in each other's company at a completely different place from that of the crime. The first student is called in and interrogated in the absence of the second, who is then interrogated in his turn (no consultation is allowed between the suspects once the interrogations have started). If their stories do not tally in every respect, their alibi is presumed false, and they are therefore 'guilty' of the crime.

In this, its classic party-game form, the activity is absorbing and motivating, with plenty of opportunity for role-play, but it is less than satisfactory as a vehicle for fluency practice. The bulk of the class has nothing to do while the two suspects are constructing their alibi; one suspect is out of it completely while the other is interrogated; and the interrogation itself can be carried on by only one student at a time, while all the others are passive.

To get over these objections, various simple modifications are possible, originally suggested by David Crookall in *Modern English Teacher* 7:1. There is no reason why there should not be three suspects instead of two; the rest of the class is then divided into three groups who prepare a battery of questions (noted down if necessary) while the suspects are getting their story ready. The suspects are then interviewed *simultaneously* on their return by the three groups; afterwards they change over, suspect A going to group B and so on, and the interrogators look for discrepancies. It is possible, but not absolutely necessary, to change over again, so that each group will have interviewed each suspect. Finally, the class collates its evidence (this constitutes the feedback session) and gives judgement.

A simpler and shorter version of this, involving only one suspect, is the *Spy* game. One member of the group is suspected of being a spy for an enemy power; he, however, claims to be a perfectly innocent citizen. The group interrogates him regarding his background, history, family, opinions etc., and he, through his answers, builds up a 'cover' for himself (not his own genuine background, of course!). By quick-fire questioning and careful noting of his answers, the group tries to catch him out in inconsistencies which will prove he is not what he says. Beyond giving the 'spy' a moment or two to think up the main lines of his story, no preparation is needed; he will make up further details as he goes along in response to questions. This exercise is, perhaps, a little difficult to explain to students, and needs a demonstration (with the teacher playing the 'spy') before being done in groups. It is a fairly short activity and needs to be performed briskly; but can be lengthened slightly by adding a rule that three inconsistencies must be found before the spy can be arrested!

Alibi is commonly used to practise the past simple and continuous tenses in their declarative, interrogative and negative forms. For example: *Where were you at 11 o'clock? How much did you pay? What were you doing when you met your friend? I paid six dollars. Why didn't you say that before?*

However, other tenses may be used, particularly in the *Spy* variation: *Do you usually act in this manner? Will you please describe . . . Where do you live? Have you always lived there?*

7   Putting in order

This task requires students to evaluate connected pieces of evidence and recognize causal, temporal or progressional relationships between them. The group is given several pictures, sentences or passages and asked to put them into some sort of logical order. If the items are complex and the criteria for ordering unclear, then the whole group may be given all the material openly, and there will still be plenty of scope for interaction. If, however, the exercise is simpler, then the combining arrangement should be used: each student is given one or two of the component ideas, which he can only describe or read out, not show. Otherwise there may be little reason for communication: the material may be pooled and one or two of the students do all the work in a moment.

No particular kind of structure or vocabulary needs revising or preparing before these exercises, beyond the obvious expressions 'comes before' or 'comes after'; the language needed is that of general negotiation, together with the subject-matter of the material given, which will vary. However, though this subject-matter itself is sometimes relatively simple, the language needed to discuss its ordering may be very advanced, depending on the subtlety of the relationships between the component parts. On the whole, the *Picture-sequence* exercise is more appropriate for younger or more elementary classes, the *Sentence-sequence* for older or more advanced ones.

Picture-sequence

In this activity each member of the group is given a picture from a series which, when properly assembled, forms a logical sequence of events or developments. Without actually displaying their

pictures to one another, students describe their contents and
thereby try to discover the correct order. In Fig. 5 (a) there is a
causal and temporal relationship between the pictures. In Fig.5 (b)
there is a story line to be uncovered; strip cartoons like this can

Fig. 5a

(from *Scientific American*)

Fig. 5b   Remember: the wolf will eat the goat, and the goat will eat the cabbage, if given the opportunity.

Fig. 5c

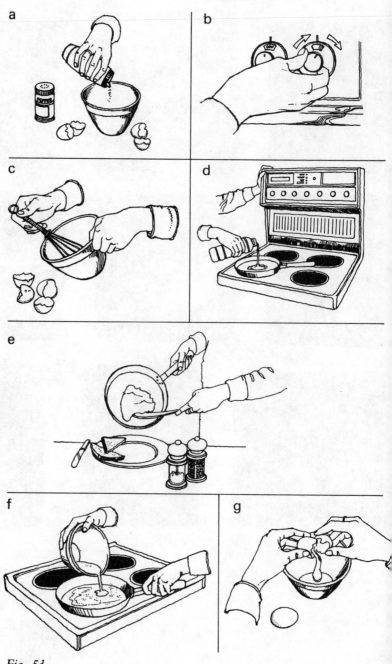

Fig. 5d

Solutions: 5a: d, a, c, b; 5b: d, f, g, b, a, c, e; 5c: d, g, b, h, f, e, c, a, i, j; 5d: g, a, c, b, d, f, e.

be taken out of newspapers or from books of short picture-stories (see *Bibliography*); there is no intrinsic reason why they should not include written dialogue (in balloons coming out of the characters' mouths for example). The task is made more challenging by increasing the number of pictures or by making the differences more subtle. In Fig.5 (c) for example the differences between some of the pictures are fairly small, though clear to us since we see them juxtaposed.

When a group is very near the solution, the temptation to 'peep' becomes overwhelming; the teacher must be on the lookout for this, and forbid participants to look at each others' pictures before the correct solution has been reached and checked. This solution may be presented in the form of a written, spoken or recorded story; or, if the pictures are number-coded, simply by the correct sequence of numbers written on a bit of paper. Then a fresh set of pictures may be given; it is wise to prepare several different sets, as groups vary greatly in the time they take to finish.

Some examples of suitable picture sequences are given in Fig. 5.

Sentence-sequence

Sentences or parts of sentences can be ordered into sequence using a very similar technique to that described above. Perhaps the most convenient way of preparing this is to take a short typed passage, cut it up and give each member of the group a sentence on a strip of paper to learn by heart. The strips of paper are then confiscated, and the group left to puzzle out the original order. For higher-level students, longer passages may be used, but not, then, learnt by heart; each student may simply read aloud his section.

I have appended a few examples of appropriate passages, but as these are not difficult to compose or find, I recommend that the teacher prepare her own, with her particular class in mind. Such passages may be simple stories – the more well-known the content, the easier they are to solve as in (a); or they may be unfamiliar anecdotes as in (b) and (c). But they may also be dialogues as in (d) and (e) or poems as in (f) and (g), or passages from novels as in (h) and (i). Non-fictional material, from newspapers for example, as in (j) calls for a higher level of sheer intellectual effort.

With some of the passages the sequence may be too obvious; the group may find the whole operation too easy and come to a quick solution without a satisfactory amount of conversation. In this case, the task needs to be made more tricky. One way of doing this is to eliminate all punctuation, as in the first and second examples. A second way is to put any conjunctions or other 'joining' words with the section before, rather than with the clause they introduce; I have done this in most of the prose examples. Thirdly, the cut-up sections may be made much shorter, and each participant be given two or three brief disconnected phrases instead of a full sentence, as in (c) below.

a) little red riding hood came along the forest path/singing happily and picking flowers as she went/but the wolf was waiting for her behind a tree/good morning little red riding hood he said smiling/good morning wolf said little red riding hood/she had forgotten that her mother had told her/she must never speak to strangers

b) my children had always wanted a pet and so when/one day we found a pigeon with a broken wing under our house/we decided to keep it and look after it/the children fed it on millet seed and kept it in an old shoe-box however/in spite of the most loving and constant care the bird died/and was given a long formal funeral

c) At noon we reached/the edge of a canyon./Thirsty, tired,/half-blinded by the sun,/we had no idea/how to proceed./ We wandered along/the edge of the precipice until/we came to a small path./ We climbed down it slowly./ Would we find water at the bottom?

d) What are you waiting for?
None of your business.
But you've been standing here for an hour.
Any law against that?
No, but I just thought . . .
Leave me alone, will you?

e) They've come!
What, already?
Yes, and they've brought the goods.
All of them?
Most of them, anyway.
Let's go and get some.
Right! Before anyone else gets there first!

f) In the gay evening
I see a long green serpent
With its tail in the dahlias.
It lies in loops across the grass
And drinks softly at the faucet.
I can hear it swallow.
(Beatrice Janosco)

g) The barber shop has curtains
    but it must have been a long time since they were washed
    for they are a dark grey
    and falling apart;
    the window itself is dirty
    and whatever signs it has are grey with dust.
    The barber stands in the doorway
    wearing a coat of uncertain white
    over dirty trousers –
    and he needs a shave badly.
    The shop is called in bold letters
    'Sanitary Barber Shop',
    And there are those, I suppose, who believe it.
    (Charles Reznikoff)

h) But why Mr Darcy came so often to the parsonage/it was more
    difficult to understand./ It could not be for society/as he
    frequently sat there/ten minutes together without opening his
    lips. And/when he did speak, it seemed/the effect of necessity
    rather than of choice,/a sacrifice to propriety/not a pleasure to
    himself.

i) So she swallowed one of the cakes and was delighted to
    find/that she began shrinking directly. As soon as /she was
    small enough to get through the door,/ she ran out of the house
    and found/quite a crowd of little animals and birds waiting
    outside./ The poor little lizard, Bill, was in the middle,/ being
    held up by two guinea pigs/ who were giving it something out
    of a bottle.

j) Mediterranean countries are expected to agree this week/on a
    multi-million pound campaign to clean up/the polluted sea that
    is the world's top tourist area./ Ministers and senior officials
    from seventeen coastal states/are meeting in Athens to put the
    finishing touches to a treaty/on controlling discharges from
    land, which are responsible for/eighty-five per cent of the
    pollution of the Mediterranean.

8 Priorities

A specific application of the concept of ordering is that of defining
priorities: I have found this one of the most fruitful bases for
discussion, in terms both of the amount of communication that
goes on, and of student involvement and enjoyment. Again,
the group is provided with a set of discrete items – usually in the

form of a list whose components may or may not be distributed among participants – and at least one criterion. They then have to order these in a scale according to how far they conform to the criterion. In real life, for example, a young couple who have bought a tumbledown cottage may make a list of what needs doing to it, in order of urgency; or a panel of judges may assess the relative merits of the contestants in a singing competition. These particular situations are difficult to simulate in the classroom, but we can easily make up parallel problems which are appropriate for our classes (see examples below).

The language used consists mostly of comparisons, and lower-level classes may benefit from a little practice in comparative and superlative constructions beforehand. In particular, the following words and phrases may be useful: *more/less important than, the most/least important, more/less than, better/worse than, as good as, not so good as, I would rather . . . , I prefer . . . , That comes above/below/before/after . . . , Which is better/more important?*

Note that the terms used in the basic list of items may be much more advanced than the language needed for the discussion, so teachers should not be put off by the apparent difficulty of the lists. Five minutes devoted to making sure that all such new lexical items are understood by all will be well worth the trouble; and by the time these have been discussed, argued over and put in a final order of priority, you may be sure that they will have been fairly thoroughly learnt!

Rating

In this first version of the 'priorities' discussion, the group has a collection of several concepts, usually expressed in words or short phrases, which all belong to one recognizable set, such as clothes, storybook characters, food. They have to rate these and put them in order of priority according to various criteria which it is most convenient to express as adjectives: tall, short, old, useful and so on. The criteria may be given to the group together with their lists, or they may not be given at all, and the students have to suggest some by themselves. On the whole, I prefer the latter system: thinking up criteria appropriate to a given set of items is in itself a good basis for preliminary discussion, and provides a warm-up to the main task of rating. Groups can be asked to find as many different criteria, with their corresponding orders of priority, as they can in a given time. A trial run with the whole class is advisable before dividing into groups.

If all the groups have been given the same criteria, then different results can be compared. There are bound to be minor variations; one group may consider as fairly important some item which another rates low in importance, and these differences may be clarified, even voted on to get a class consensus. If, however, no criteria have been openly set, the feedback can be given by each group reading out one of its resulting orders, and getting the others to guess what the criterion was (surprisingly difficult!).

Here are some instances of suitable sets of items, with some suggestions for criteria. These examples themselves are already listed in an ascending scale, the criterion being in this case a combination of language-level and age of participants. One or two are somewhat culture-bound, *Heroes* for example, or the last item of *Ways of getting money;* teachers may need to change these to suit the background of their students.

Foods: meat, tomatoes, bananas, chocolate, bread, water, cake, oil, rice.
Criteria: essential to life, sweet, cheap, healthy, fattening.

Animals: dragon, shark, elephant, snake, crocodile, tiger, wolf.
Criteria: dangerous, large, beautiful, strong, common.

Famous people: Charlie Chaplin, Hitler, Napoleon, Leonardo da Vinci, Cleopatra, King Solomon.
Criteria: famous, good, powerful, popular, ancient.

Clothes: boots, coat, jeans, belt, gloves, hat, shirt.
Criteria: useful, expensive, comfortable, warm, decorative.

Means of transport: ship, yacht, plane, bus, car, lorry, helicopter, hovercraft.
Criteria: speedy, comfortable, heavy, noisy, costly, useful.

Colours: red, yellow, purple, green, orange, white, black, brown.
Criteria: cheerful, dark, warm, restful, fashionable, practical.

Leisure activities: swimming, dancing, walking, reading, sleeping, stamp-collecting, going to the theatre, listening to music, drinking (beer, wine etc.).
Criteria: educational, refreshing, restful, healthy, enjoyable, productive, sociable.

School subjects: biology, art, literature, mathematics, music, psychology, foreign languages, cooking.
Criteria: useful, difficult, interesting, creative.

Heroes: Superman, Prometheus, Samson, Sherlock Holmes, Davy Crockett, Peter Pan, Robin Hood.
Criteria: old, handsome, sexy, intelligent, admirable.

Ways of getting people to do what you want: persuasion, request, flattery, torture, bribery, command, threats.
Criteria: effective, violent, common, pleasant, quick.

Ways of getting money: bank robbery, tax evasion, hard work, inheriting a fortune, speculation, marrying a rich wife/husband, winning the pools.
Criteria: efficient, ethical, difficult, reliable.

Survival games

In comparison with most of the other 'priorities' tasks, survival games are less abstract, and demand less of an intellectual effort; they are based on dramatic, urgent situations, and the discussion, though not too demanding, is complex and absorbing. The idea is that the group, in an isolated situation cut off from civilization, has to decide which of a given list of items are most essential for their survival and return home, and to place them in order of priority.

The *N.A.S.A. Game* is easily the most well-known of these. It was originally designed as an exercise in group decision-making (in the native language) and is widely used in this way (see Pfeiffer and Jones, *Bibliography*). However, it can be equally effective as a foreign language discussion activity. It runs like this: the group has landed on the moon, but has become separated from the main party at the base, and has 200 miles to cover in order to reach it. The following items are available, to be numbered in order of necessity for survival:

box of matches (15)
food concentrate (4)
50 feet of nylon rope (6)
parachute silk (8)
portable heating unit (13)
two 45-calibre pistols (11)
one case of dehydrated
   milk (12)
two 100-pound tanks of
   oxygen (1)

map of the stars as seen from
   the moon (3)
life-raft (9)
magnetic compass (14)
five gallons of water (2)
signal flares (10)
first-aid kit (7)
solar-powered receiver-
   transmitter (5)

The numbers in brackets indicate the solution suggested by N.A.S.A. In the original game, each participant is given a duplicate copy of the above list (without numbers!), and marks down his own order of priority, using numbers as above (one for the most important item, fifteen for the least). Then all the group together discuss the list and try to come to unanimous agreement on an order; they compare their results with those of the other groups, and discuss differences. After that they return to their own groups and go through the whole process again and even again until the whole class reaches a final solution. This may then be compared with N.A.S.A.'s own suggested answers.

I would suggest various modifications to this if we are to use it as a basis for foreign language discussion. A preliminary session of a few minutes' teaching is necessary to make sure all items are understood; then participants should be given a short time to try to define their priorities individually, each one numbering the items on his paper accordingly. This should be stopped as soon as the first student or two finish; it is not, as in the original game, essential for each student to have a complete definitive order of his own before beginning to talk; the purpose of this part of the activity is simply to familiarize students with the names of the items and get them to start thinking about the issues involved. As soon as one or two are ready, the group discussions may begin. In the original game it is explicitly stipulated that the group must come to unanimous agreement; anyone who disagrees may not give in or be overruled – he must persuade or be persuaded. In principle, this is a very productive condition, in that it ensures careful and thorough exploration of every difference of opinion; but if taken to extremes it may hold up the final execution of the task intolerably; we may therefore allow an occasional majority vote if unanimity seems unattainable.

Two kinds of feedback session are possible: one is to have a full class discussion to try to come to a general definitive solution; the other is simply to give the answers suggested by N.A.S.A. and see which group was nearest. The first is fun, but it can be long-drawn-out and has the usual disadvantage of full class discussions: relatively little individual participation. The second is quicker, but may be something of a let-down; students will want to protest, support their own versions, discuss further. Of course, one can combine the two: try to reach a full class consensus, and if it looks like taking too long, give the N.A.S.A. version. On the whole, if the group discussions have been very long and thorough, then the summing-up can be brief; if they have been short and relatively superficial, then the class may benefit from a general debate.

The *N.A.S.A. game* is meant for fairly adult groups. Other similar exercises may be made more suitable for younger students by basing them on less remote locations and simpler lists of equipment. Here are some examples:

In the middle of the ocean: small boat or raft, matches, signal-flares, oars, oil-lamp with oil, telescope, map of the ocean, knife, life-belts, string, water, tent, blankets, compass, fish-hooks.

In the Sahara desert: six packets of cigarettes, ten blankets, map of North Africa, ten metres of rope, watch, sack of dried dates and figs, oil-stove with supply of oil, two pencils, knife, magnifying glass, three jerry-cans of water, two stretchers, hats, some old newspapers.

At the North Pole: thirty kilos of canned food, twenty metres of rope, ten signal flares, inflatable raft, six pairs of sunglasses, jerry-can of water (frozen), twenty boxes of matches, bottle of brandy, small sledge, small first-aid kit, large number of blankets, gas cooker with gas, magnetic compass, battery-run transistor radio.

Trapped underground: twenty metres of nylon climbing-rope, spade, battery-run transistor radio, torch, pick, small amount of explosives with detonator, spare batteries for torch, jerry-can of water, watch, coats and warm clothing for each person, cigarette-lighter, magnetic compass, protective helmets, first-aid kit, chalk.

Features and functions

More abstract, but not more difficult, is to rate personal character-istics in order of their importance for a given role or job. This can be the follow-up to a brainstorming session as suggested in *Qualities,* (p. 36), but the process is usually more clear-cut if an arbitrary list of such features is given. For example, how would you rate the following qualities in a colleague at work: nice appearance, friendliness, even temper, sense of humour, cooperativeness, responsibility, expertise at job? Personally, I would rate them more or less in the reverse order to that in which I have written them, but the reader will probably disagree: plenty of scope for discussion here.

The general organization of this exercise is similar to that of the *Survival games,* but of course assessment of the relative merits of the items is far more subjective, far more dependent on the background and personalities of the students: it is therefore virtually impossible to suggest a 'right' solution. However, I have found it a good idea for the teacher to work out her own order in advance, and let students know she has done so. This is partly because the knowledge that she has done this encourages students to try their own hand at it; and partly because her list does supply some sort of yardstick with which to compare their own results at the end, without necessarily implying that either version is right or wrong.

Again, the material should be presented in the form of duplicated lists which students may be allowed to mark, with possibly one extra copy to be filled in with the final group solution. Examples are given below; I have found it more practical to express the features as adjectives or verbs, than as abstract nouns. Teachers should make sure their students know how to treat these structures; it might be useful to teach 'base' phrases such as *A mother-in-law should (be)* . . . *,* or *It is (more) important for a mother-in-law to (be)* . . .

It is as well to choose a subject students are likely to feel they know something about; the *teacher,* for example, is a good one to start with and usually goes well.

Teacher: intelligent, pleasant to look at, consistent, moral in private life, fair, honest, authoritative, flexible, has sense of humour, loves children, makes lessons interesting, knows subject, teaches subject well, speaks clearly.

Wife or husband: tolerant, considerate, faithful, affectionate to husband/wife, affectionate to children, hardworking, tidy, home-loving, good-looking, rich, thrifty, quiet, well-educated.

Ruler: just, knowledgeable, rich, honest, married, authoritative, charismatic, friendly, hard-working, clever, eloquent, confident, tolerant, tall, has well-ordered private life.

Baby (one year to eighteen months old): beautiful, toilet-trained, affectionate, obedient, quiet, healthy, cheerful, sociable with strangers, intelligent for its age, sleeps through the night, eats well, can play alone for long periods.

Mother-in-law: willing to baby-sit, attractive, generous, young (relatively!), well-dressed, rich, good at organizing home, has telephone, has many interests, does not interfere, has other married children, lives nearby.

Soldier (a private): disciplined, strong, brave, well-trained, patriotic, intelligent, resourceful, healthy, educated, even-tempered, tidy, cheerful, friendly, shoots accurately, thinks for himself.

9 Choosing candidates (a)

This is another exercise which requires assessment and comparison, but here participants are asked to choose only one item (usually a human candidate) for a certain purpose. This needs more teacher-preparation than most of the other activities described here, because the group must have before it detailed information about the relative merits of each candidate: their personal backgrounds, needs, tastes, characters, qualifications; and because such a large amount of information cannot be committed to memory, it has to be set out in the form of a written memorandum, a copy of which is given to each participant.

There is much scope for role-play here; the most convenient setting is a committee meeting. Each member of the committee may or may not have an individual role (of profession, function or personality); and the candidates themselves may be role-played where necessary, urging their own claims, or arguing among themselves as to their respective merits.

The decision should ideally be taken with the full agreement of every participant (except, if present, the candidates themselves); and a lot of arguing and convincing will be needed in order to achieve this. If in spite of all its efforts the group fails to attain unanimity, a majority vote may be taken.

There is often considerable variation in the rates at which different groups perform this task; a group which finishes quickly may be asked to select a second reserve candidate, or even a third. At the end the decisions of each group are brought before all the others and, if it is wished, a short full class discussion may ensue to try to sum up and arrive at a general consensus.

This exercise is suitable for classes of mature students rather than young schoolchildren; and in order to work it has to be taken fairly seriously. No particular language preparation is needed, beyond a check that the information sheets are thoroughly understood. Many different language functions may be needed (persuading, advising, agreeing, disagreeing, comparing, evaluating, requesting information, providing information) and the number of different structures needed is correspondingly large.

Prize-winners

Choosing a candidate for some academic award is a fairly relevant subject for most of our students. Here is an example: there is a meeting of the University Appointments Committee. On the agenda is the awarding of this year's Law Scholarship. Five students have attained similar marks in the entrance exam. They have all applied for the scholarship, which includes full tuition fees and upkeep for the three-year course leading to a degree in law at the University.

This can be done perfectly well 'straight', that is to say with students expressing their own genuine opinions; or it can be done using role-play, where each member of the committee has his or her own axe to grind. Some possible roles are: the head of the law faculty, the representative of the benefactor who endowed the scholarship, a representative of the student council, a law professor, a professional lawyer, the treasurer, a local politician, a housewife. Here is the information sheet:

Albert Smith Aged 37, not of outstanding natural ability but very hard-working. Married with three children; until now a taxi driver. His applying was probably due largely to his wife's ambition. Albert made a good impression, but seems a little nervous at the whole idea of law-school and the effects his new career might have on his social life and family. If he fails the scholarship he will go back to taxi-driving.

Basil Katz Aged 19, brilliant but not very hard-working. A likeable personality, of left-wing sympathies, has taken part in some more or less violent demonstrations and has been in prison at least once as a result. Lots of girlfriends, has a reputation for treating them badly. Very musical, has founded and runs a pop-group. Will probably make this his career if he fails the scholarship, which would be a 'terrible waste' according to his school tutor who recommends him.

Carole Andersen Aged 20, a quiet, attractive girl, responsible and able, but rather pliable in character, engaged to be married to a doctor, would like to finish her University studies before settling down. Her fiancé says: 'I want Carole to fulfil herself in every way, but of course once she is married, home and children will occupy her first and foremost.' Her parents cannot afford to finance the course.

Daphne Braun Aged 21, single, the daughter and granddaughter of lawyers. Enthusiastically Women's Lib., ambitious and career-minded. Academic record erratic, some very good results, some mediocre. Had a mental breakdown last year, was in hospital for three months but appears to have made a complete recovery. Fined recently for being in possession of marijuana. Parents cannot finance her studies. In character rather aggressive and quick-tempered, but generous, a good friend.

Edward Mbaka Aged 24, has been in the Army and seen active service. Divorced, no family. Highly motivated, wants eventually to go into politics. 'I want this course more than anything,' he says, 'and only the scholarship can get it for me.' While in the army he was once found guilty of accepting bribes. Charming personality, fluent and eloquent speaker. A citizen of this country, but retains also the nationality of his native African state, to which he may eventually return.

Heirs

Another possibility is the ever interesting question of legacies and heirs. In the following exercise the group is a committee appointed by the court to decide who should get the valuable estate of Lord Moulton, who made no will and has no direct heirs. The law gives no ruling (for the purposes of this activity, anyway!), and it is up to the committee to decide to whom the money should go. The estate may not be divided.

Some role-play characters on the committee: an old friend of Lord Moulton's, a local shopkeeper, a social worker, the local clergyman, a judge, a socialist member of the local council, a conservative member of the local council. These are the claimants:

Lady Searle Lord Moulton's widowed cousin, his only living relative, aged 66, living alone in a small village in comfortable but not luxurious circumstances. The money would enable her to hire a nurse (she is often ill), travel, move into pleasanter surroundings. She has no immediate family, is not very popular in her neighbourhood. Has not been on speaking terms with Lord Moulton for years, following a quarrel.

Miss Langland The nurse who attended Lord Moulton for the last four years of his life, 48 years old, loves her work and is professionally very able. Was very well-paid by Lord Moulton, and her savings will enable her to take a long holiday before taking up another similar post. An affectionate and loyal attendant, she undoubtedly eased Lord Moulton's latter years.

Tim Brodie The son of Lord Moulton's gardener. Lord Moulton took a liking to him, paid for his education and took a constant interest in his welfare. Tim, who has a flair for languages, desperately wants to study abroad, but has no money so will have to get a job and save if he can. An attractive and popular young man, drives a motorbike much too fast, lots of girlfriends, not very honest.

Jane Smith A penniless young unmarried woman with a small baby who has recently appeared on the scene claiming to be Lord Moulton's daughter. Has a letter which appears to be in Lord Moulton's writing and signed by him, addressed to her mother (now dead) admitting paternity and proposing marriage. Refuses to give any further details of her past life, and has no references.

The local orphanage A charity which receives no help from the State, though new legislation might change this. It has occasionally received donations from Lord Moulton in the past and is certainly badly in need of funds. However, it is badly run, and there is a possibility that much of the money might find its way into the pockets of officials rather than being used for the orphans.

Prisoners

Another variation is to choose the least undeserving of the candidates rather than the most deserving. Let us imagine, for example, that a number of petty criminals have been convicted and sent to prison. They have all applied to be set free on probation; if this is granted then they will resume their normal life but will have to report to the police at fixed intervals, and will certainly go to prison if they commit any further offences. Their applications were at first refused, but the local prison is so overcrowded that at least one of them will have to go on probation after all. Which one?

John Barker Aged 22, unmarried. A pickpocket with one previous conviction. Clever, a skilled carpenter, but very unstable personality, moves quickly from job to job and girl to girl. Rather conceited, likes to boast about his thefts, but likeable.

May Croft Aged 25, married with two children, found guilty of shoplifting. Tried to plead mental instability (kleptomania) but psychiatric examination did not support this. Says she loves her children, but constantly neglects them; they are being looked after by mother-in-law. Not on good terms with her husband.

Brad Jackson Aged 20, unmarried, seriously injured a man in a drunken fight over a girl. Says he regretted it afterwards, blames it on drink. Often drunk and violent. No job, lives with his widowed mother who is much distressed but has no control over him. Hates prison, will do anything to get out.

Barbara Howard Aged 21, unmarried, smuggled diamonds and watches, had been doing so for some months before being caught. Daughter of rich and respected family, claims she did it for 'kicks'. Associates with rather wild, party-going, drug-taking set, has used drugs herself, but not addicted. No permanent boyfriend, probably promiscuous. Shocked parents have disowned her.

Bob Mikes Aged 37, married with three children, two at school. Worked in office, found out boss was having affair with secretary, blackmailed him. When his demands became too high and he threatened physical violence if not paid, his employer told police. Mikes' wife claims she knew nothing. One previous conviction ten years ago for theft.

Simon Patten Aged 20, junior member of Mafia-style protection racket that threatened small shopkeepers if they did not pay up. Has girlfriend, wants to get married, promises will go straight. Does he mean it? Protection-racket boss (unidentified) has reportedly said he will 'look after him' and 'find him a job' when he comes out, if he tells no tales.

Victims

The situation can of course be reversed, and the one to be chosen can be a candidate for misfortune rather than reward. In the above exercise, for example, we could say that the prison is so overcrowded that five of the criminals will have to be released on probation: who will be detained? Or let us take the situation in ancient Athens before the advent of Theseus, when a certain number of young people had to be sent to be devoured by the Minotaur every year. All but one of them have been chosen and the last is to be one of five girls: which is least worth saving? The usual system of casting lots has been discarded in favour of decision by a committee of elders (the group). *Note:* the names and general atmosphere are Greek, but details of the girls' background do not necessarily conform with what is known of Athenian culture!

Chloe One of six brothers and sisters, family very influential, so children have so far escaped being sent. Chloe is very talented, has won several prizes for singing and music. Engaged to be married to rich businessman who threatens to withdraw financial support from the government if Chloe is sent.

Arete Only child, mentally retarded but adored by parents. Occasionally violent, once attacked young child through jealousy but parents have seen to it that this should not recur. Occupies herself with simple sewing jobs.

Charis Orphan, rather a wild character, has lived on the streets, kept alive by charity and occasional thieving. Has recently come to live with a middle-class family, responding well to affection and teaching; shows signs of exceptional intellect.

Thalia One of five children, but her brother was sent last year. Thalia was very close to him and wants to be sent, hoping he may still be alive, but her parents are naturally violently opposed to her going. Very popular, an excellent athlete.

Euphro Eldest of six brothers and sisters, the family is fairly well-off. Ugly, nobody likes her very much as she is intolerant and given to unkind gossip. Mother often ill, so Euphro spends much of her time looking after younger brothers and sisters.

This discussion may seem rather brutal, so we can, at the end, announce to the class that in fact nobody was eaten: Theseus saved them all!

10   Choosing candidates (b)

In a more sophisticated and creative version of *Choosing candidates* the background and claims of the candidates are made up by the students themselves.

Four of the students are appointed to the committee or 'panel of judges'; the rest are divided into groups of three or four, each comprising a candidate and his supporters. The committee is to award a certain named prize, and the supporters have to devise as original and convincing reasons as possible in favour of their candidate getting it. For ten to fifteen minutes the supporters and candidates plan their cases, with as much background detail as possible, while the committee of judges discusses what sort of candidate they are looking for, and what questions they will ask. Finally the judges interview the candidates – singly or simultaneously – and decide who is the winner.

Some possible prizes and how to win them:

– £10,000 for three years. The winner must propose the most interesting/constructive/persuasive plan for how he/she will use the money and spend the time.

– Man/Woman of the Year Award. The winner must have had the most impressive (imaginary) achievements over the past twelve months.

– A fortnight's free holiday, no expense spared. The winner must give the most original, attractive description of the holiday he wants.

– The job of President, Prime Minister, or the equivalent, of the

students' country. The winner must put forward the most
promising programme of internal reforms and foreign policy.

– Three wishes. The winner must suggest the most original and
effective use of the wishes.

11   Layout problems

These again are exercises involving some preliminary reading, and
are suitable for mature, advanced students. A set of people or
animals are to be arranged in some sort of layout – round a table,
for example, or in a set of dwelling-places – which has to take into
account various limitations, relationships or individual quirks:
that A cannot be near B, or that nobody likes C, for instance.
There is not necessarily one right answer; on the contrary, a result
which comprises ideal solutions to all the problems may be
impossible, and the group should be told to aim for a sensible
compromise (as is usual in real life!).

The basic procedure is similar to that of *Choosing candidates*.
Each member of the group is given a copy of the information
sheet with details of the characters, their problems, and a map or
plan; pencils and rough paper should also be available. It is a good
idea for the teacher to read the text aloud before the students
begin talking, explaining any difficult expressions as she goes.
Besides helping them with the language, this also gives
participants an initial general impression of the issues involved, so
that they will spend less time on preliminary reading, and
correspondingly more on talking. About twenty minutes should
then be allowed for discussion, during which groups try to
arrive at a reasonable solution. In the feedback, one group may
display their proposed final layout on a blackboard or an overhead
projector, to be criticized or improved in the light of other
groups' ideas; or all groups may display their results simultaneously, to be compared and assessed; or the teacher may propose
her own solution, justify it, and invite comments.

The teacher should study the text of the information sheet
carefully before the lesson, think about the implications of all the
conditions, and work out how she would solve the problem.
For this activity, rather more teacher guidance is needed during
the course of the talking than in other previously-described
activities; students do not always realize the full implications of
the problems or remember to take them all into account. The
teacher needs to go from group to group, clarifying, reminding,
'throwing spanners in the works' ('Have you thought about

. . . ?' 'Yes, but your solution doesn't account for . . .' 'A good idea, except for this corner – look who you've put with X!'). For the feedback too she will need to be familiar with the material in order to be able to appreciate students' solutions and make proposals of her own. With the careful preparation that makes such involvement possible, the teacher can contribute a great deal to student understanding, involvement and enjoyment. This preparation, moreover, though time-consuming, is a good investment: if the teacher has made enough extra copies of the information sheet and studied the problems thoroughly once, she will have nothing further to prepare for re-plays with other classes.

Three variations of this exercise are given here: *Zoo plan, Couples,* and *Dinner party.* Each has its own layout sketch and information sheet for reproduction; I have also appended to each one further notes for the teacher, amplifying and clarifying some of the issues, and a possible solution.

Zoo plan

This is the least sophisticated of the three exercises presented here; the issues are fairly straightforward, and younger students should be able to do it successfully, provided their English is good enough. Each student has a plan of the present layout of the zoo and a list of problems or new developments which necessitate changes. They discuss the situation and try to arrive at a new layout which will solve all the problems.

INFORMATION SHEET

1. The giraffe is about to give birth.
2. One of the lions has died.
3. Small children are alarmed by seeing the crocodiles facing them as they come in.
4. The zoo has recently been given a new panda.
5. The monkeys are very noisy, disturbing animals.
6. The camel is rather smelly.
7. All the enclosures should be filled.
8. Harmless animals should not be put next to predators (other animals which could attack and/or eat them in the natural state).
9. The zoo has enough money to buy two wolves *or* four flamingoes *or* a pair of small deer.

TEACHER'S NOTES

The above items each necessitate some move or moves; students

Layout of zoo

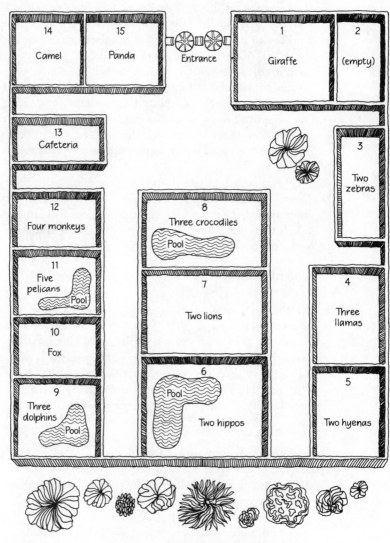

Fig. 6

should be able to work these out for themselves, but they may overlook something. Here are explicit details:

1. The giraffe should be moved away from the noisy entrance.
2. The remaining lion should be moved into a smaller enclosure.
3. The crocodiles must be moved (remember they need a pool).
4. Two pandas will need a bigger enclosure.
5. The monkeys should not be near the cafeteria, nor next to quiet creatures like the pelicans who may be disturbed by them.
6. The camel should not be near the cafeteria!

Zoo (possible solution)

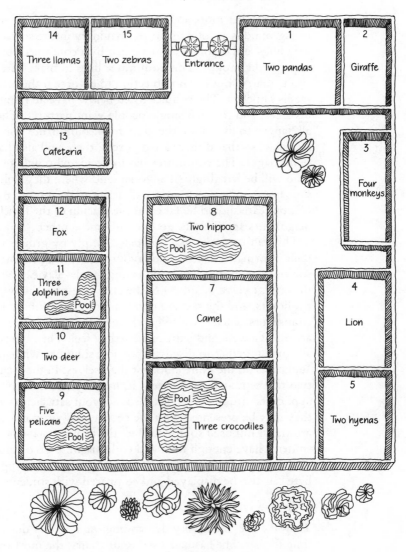

7. The zoo will have to buy one of the items mentioned in 9.
8. The hyenas should not be next to the llamas, nor should the fox be near the pelicans.
9. If the wolves are bought, an enclosure must be found next to animals they would not frighten; the flamingoes would need a pool; and the deer may not be put next to predators.

This activity was suggested by a listening comprehension exercise presented in a lecture by Alan Maley.

Couples

This is a rather more sophisticated problem for adult students. Its background is as follows: in an imaginary future society, all weddings and divorces are arranged by a committee of marriage experts (the group). This committee likes to make sure that all adults marry, but has no objection to divorce if the relationship seems hopeless. The couples listed below have all requested divorces, and the two single people want partners. They all happen to live along the same road. No further houses are available, so that if there are divorces, there will also have to be remarriages. The committee has to decide who will get a divorce, who will be left single (if anyone), and where they will all live. One house may be left empty if all the applicants are paired off; but care should be taken in the placing of the families so that neighbours are likely to get on with one another.

This can be done, like *Zoo plan,* simply by groups discussing their information-sheets and layouts, and trying to suggest a solution; or, if the class is big enough, role-play can be used. In this case, twelve members of the class role-play the twelve applicants, and the rest are divided into pairs of marriage counsellors. Each couple visit three or four pairs of counsellors, are interviewed, and explain how they feel. Then the counsellors all come together to discuss a possible solution, while the applicants do the same amongst themselves. In the feedback, the two results may be compared. If, however, as is likely, the applicants' group fails to arrive at a layout satisfactory to all, then they may be presented with the counsellors' proposal as an arbitrary, imposed solution. Here the activity may end, unless students have enough time and enthusiasm to go on arguing until a class consensus is reached. If wished, the solution suggested here can also be displayed and compared with students' proposals.

INFORMATION SHEET

Tony and Sue She is very demanding, he is a busy doctor with no time for her. She has had a string of affairs, the most recent with Martin. Tony complains she wastes his money, she says he is stingy. No children. She is bored, spends her time shopping and at parties.

Martin and Rachel Martin has been having an affair with Sue, which he has made no effort to hide. Rachel still loves him, but is deeply hurt by his selfishness and unfaithfulness. There is one six-year-old child. Martin is an architect, good at his work, a good father. She is a teacher, but her home situation is affecting her work badly.

Jerry and Ada A rich couple. She has had a mental breakdown and is in hospital, but they had decided to separate before this. She has depressions and is difficult to live with. She won't give parties or be polite to his business colleagues: this is bad for his career. He married her for her good looks, soon regretted it, and has had several discreet affairs.

Bert and Cathy He is a bus driver, she is a nurse. They are by now on very bad terms, quarrel all the time. He is affectionate, home-loving and conventional, wants her to be a good housewife. She loves her work, is always at the hospital. No children: he wants, she doesn't.

Larry and Edith They have three children, but have been virtually separated (though living in the same house) for two years. Edith is fully occupied being a housewife and mother, Larry is a clerk in an office. The children are disturbed and problematic. Larry has been in love with Ada for many years, but has not tried to approach her, for moral and religious reasons. He is stable, but rather stuffy and conventional.

Nina Young, attractive, well-dressed, capable, wants to be a lawyer, mainly because of the social status this will give her; but it is doubtful if she has the patience to study.

Will Aged 30, a widower. He is an explorer, constantly going off on dramatic, rather dangerous expeditions. Would like a wife, but cannot promise any kind of stable home life; does not want children.

TEACHER'S NOTES

Students may be reminded to consider the following questions: Is this marriage worth saving? If so, how can the couple be helped? If not, what sort of new husband/wife is needed for each partner, and is such a character available? How will the children have the best chance of a stable, affectionate home? How important is it for them to be with their parents? Will there be friction if ex-wives and husbands, or lovers, live next door to each other? If a couple are divorced, which partner should stay in the original house? Or should they both move?

My solution (by no means the only, or 'right', one) can be justified as follows: Tony, the busy doctor, and Cathy, the busy nurse, seem made for one another; if Tony really is stingy, this will matter less, as Cathy has her own income. Sue needs an exciting challenge in her life, perhaps accompanying Will on his expeditions will give it to her; she probably wouldn't make a very good mother anyway. Rachel and Martin still have a good

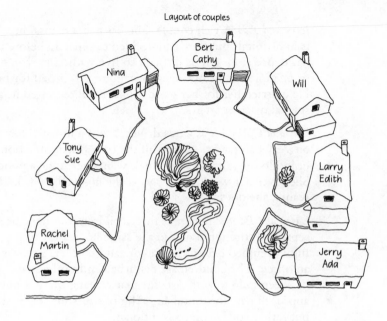

Layout of couples

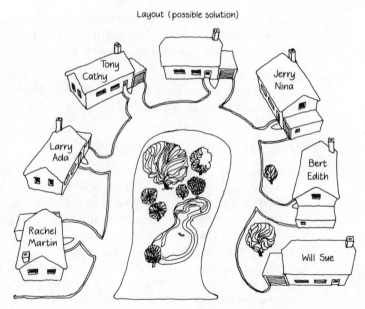

Layout (possible solution)

Fig. 7

chance of rebuilding their relationship, based on Rachel's affection and their child; marriage guidance is probably needed. Jerry wants an ambitious, capable wife – Nina is suitable, and will find the social position she wants with him. Ada may find stability and affection with Larry. Bert will be a good father to Edith's children and she will give him the home he craves.

86

Dinner party

This is also for adults. It goes as follows: Mr and Mrs Smith are giving a dinner party which they are eager should be a success, but it turns out that they have a varied, rather tricky selection of guests. They have a long, narrow dinner table; Mr Smith will sit at one end and Mrs Smith at the other. But how should they seat the other twelve guests so that there will be general pleasant conversation and no excitement, embarrassment or friction? Mrs Smith asked her new social secretary to make a seating plan, but the layout she (the secretary) suggested is far from satisfactory. Mrs Smith has now applied to a firm specializing in social relations (the group) to suggest a suitable arrangement. Her instructions are given in the *Information sheet*.

Groups work out their suggested arrangements using the original seating plan as a basis. However, it will be found that, once familiar with the various characters, participants are likely to jettison the original plan completely and start from scratch. This is quite legitimate; the first version is only there to illustrate some of the problems and familiarize participants with the names.

When solutions have been suggested, these may be compared or combined into a final class version. One amusing follow-up is to invite members of the class to select roles from among the characters given and say whether they are happy or not about where they are sitting, and why. Another is to test out the solution in a more practical manner: fourteen students are selected to role-play the characters, seated according to the suggested solution, and invited to act out the dinner party itself.

INFORMATION SHEET

1. Mr and Mrs Smith should sit opposite each other at the ends of the table. Apart from this, members of the same family should not sit next to or directly opposite each other.
2. Men and women should be seated alternately round the table.
3. Amy Eliot and Colin Smith are violently in love.
4. Jennifer Harvey, a professor, and colleague of Mr Smith, can tell amusing stories, but is rather anti-semitic.
5. Lady Margaret Eliot is very correct, polite and boring.
6. Judge Masters is a good listener, very tactful.
7. Father O'Neil loves to give advice.
8. Rabbi Simons loves to argue, but is never offensive.
9. Old Mrs Smith talks a lot, is a bit stupid and rather deaf.
10. Mr Chasuble is extremely right-wing in his views.
11. Mrs Chasuble has very bad table-manners and is always complaining.

12. Mary Smith is rather spoilt and impatient, often rude to her parents and grandmother.
13. Sir Alan Eliot is a Socialist politician, very interested in social issues.
14. Mrs Smith does not like Mr Chasuble.
15. Mr Smith cannot stand Lady Eliot.

TEACHER'S NOTES

As it is very difficult to solve all these problems, students should be encouraged to weigh up their relative importance; a situation which may lead to slight embarrassment, for instance, may have to be accepted if it helps to avoid a situation of outright friction. Some of the items in the *Information sheet* may need amplifying.

1. Note that there are three families to which this applies: the Smiths, the Chasubles and the Eliots.
3. Does this mean that they should be put together or kept apart? Up to the students!
4. She should not be put near the Rabbi!
5. Don't put her by people who might offend her sense of propriety (Mrs Chasuble? Mary Smith?).
6. Can be near anyone – use him to neutralize the more 'difficult' characters (Mary Smith, old Mrs Smith, the Chasubles).
7. Might be able to give advice to the young girls, or Mrs Chasuble.
8. Find someone congenial for him to argue with!
9. A difficult character – be careful who you put her with.
10. Don't put him too near Sir Alan!
11. She needs someone who will listen to her or distract her from her complaints.
12. So don't put her near her parents or grandmother!
13. As he is a socialist, he certainly won't get on with Mr Chasuble, and may not feel at ease with Father O'Neil.

The solution suggested here can be explained as follows: Father O'Neil will sympathize with and advise the querulous Mrs Chasuble; or she may be distracted by Professor Harvey's anecdotes. Mr Smith and Professor Harvey can always talk about their work. The lovers will talk to each other mostly; but Colin may be distracted by his other neighbour's stories, and Amy and Mary might have common interests (being of similar age, both connected with Colin). Judge Masters will cope tactfully with Mr Chasuble's extremist views, and with old Mrs Smith's deafness, volubility and silliness. He can also talk to Mary if her other neighbours are occupied. Lady Margaret can be trusted to behave

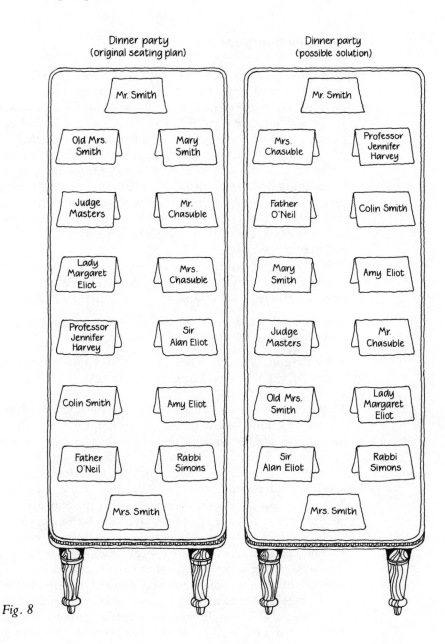

Dinner party
(original seating plan)

Dinner party
(possible solution)

Fig. 8

towards old Mrs Smith with forbearance, and not to let herself be offended by Mr Chasuble. Sir Alan and the Rabbi will probably get into warm discussion on social issues, but their hostess is on the spot to make sure this does not get too heated.

12   Combining versions

This activity begins rather like *Picture differences* (p. 52), in that
two students sit opposite one another and try to detect
discrepancies between their different versions, without actually
seeing any but their own. But here, texts are used instead of
pictures; and the identification of differences is only the
preliminary. The main task before students is to compare the
different variations and decide which is right, on the basis
of common sense and consistency. Naturally, no one of the given
texts will be completely right or wrong, so that each discrepancy
will have to be assessed separately. When all the mistakes have
been corrected, the students should be left with a coherent
and logical passage.

Here is a brief example of what I mean: the two versions of the
opening sentence of *Plans for a trip* (the full texts of this and
other similar pairs of versions are given at the end of this section).

– We are going to take a family of about five students on a
  cycling trip to the Himalayas for one week.

– We are going to take a small group of about fifty students on a
  boating trip to central France for two weeks.

Now at first there is nothing to tell participants which of the first
variations ('family'/'small group') is right; but the following
'five students'/'fifty students' make it clear: 'family' is appropriate
to neither and may be eliminated. If 'small group' is left then
'five students' is obviously more suitable than fifty. So we may
adopt 'a small group of about five students'. They could be
cycling or boating; but the latter fits neither the Himalayas nor
central France; and one would not consider the Himalayas suitable
cycling terrain, so we are left with the more likely 'cycling trip
to central France'. As to the 'one week'/'two weeks', we have no
way of knowing which is right at this stage, and only the last
sentence of the text, which gives the dates of the trip, will tell us.

To prepare pairs of texts like this is quite tricky and has to be
done carefully, so that the solution is neither too obvious nor too
difficult. It is best to take a paragraph or two of some passage
of prose that is of the appropriate level of difficulty for the class,
and go through it marking variations – one or two to a line –
above the words of the original. Then each version is copied out
separately, distributing right and wrong variations fairly
equally between them, and duplicated to the required number. All
the wrong variations should be mistakes of *content* (as in the
example given above), able to be corrected with certainty only by

reference to the other version (and hence, by interaction with the partner); mistakes of grammar, punctuation and spelling are pointless for the purpose of this activity, as they can be corrected individually.

The pair-organization of this activity, as I have said, is similar to that of *Picture differences;* but here, students may be allowed to mark their corrections onto the original texts – there is no other way of doing it, really, short of copying out the whole thing. It is possible to seat students in fours, with two students sharing a text; this is advisable if they are lacking in confidence or not very fluent. The teacher does not, in this exercise, read the passages aloud beforehand; the language and content should not be difficult enough to render this necessary (anything not understood can be explained individually); and anyway, part of the student interaction consists of communicating the content of the texts by reading aloud and verbal description. She should, however, advise students to read through the whole passage before starting to compare in detail, since it may only become apparent which of the first variations are right through comparison with something later on (as in the example quoted above); and she should emphasize, too, that they may on no account show each other their texts; everything must be communicated by word of mouth.

At the end, one student may read out his finished version, to be approved or corrected by the others; or the correct solution may be given by the teacher. Further similar exercises should be kept in reserve for use by students who finish the first passage quickly.

Usually, as implied above, there will be two versions converging on one correct solution (as in *Fairy story* and *Plans for a trip* below). However, it is possible, though more complicated, to prepare three such versions for student-groups of three or six (*Information about a journey*). Finally, pairs of versions can be prepared that have not one right answer but two; they are simply two parallel texts that have got mixed up and need to be disentangled (*In a shop* and *A letter*); these can be amusing, as the examples will show. Correct solutions are appended to help the teacher check students' results.

Fairy story

FAIRY STORY (MIXED-UP VERSION A)

Once upon a time there was a beautiful princess who lived with her old father, the prince, in a distant land. She was kind and good, but very sad; she so wanted to be beautiful, and was afraid

no handsome man would ever love and marry her. One day as she
was walking round her room, she met an old man who was as
ugly as she. 'Good morning, my lovely,' said the princess.
'Oh no,' laughed the princess, 'I am not lovely, I wish I were!'
'Your soul is beautiful, my child,' said the man. 'Take this magic
flower, and it will make your face as lovely as your heart.' She
then went away, and the astonished princess put the ring on her
finger. She immediately became as beautiful as the woman,
and many princes asked her hand in marriage. But in the end, she
refused them all, became a housewife and ruled the land well
and happily for many years.

FAIRY STORY (MIXED-UP VERSION B)

Once upon a time there was an ugly queen who lived with her old
husband, the king, in a distant land. She was happy and good,
but very ill; she so wanted to be clever, and was afraid no
handsome prince would ever love and marry her. One day as she
was walking near the palace, she met an old woman who was
as ugly as she. 'Good morning, my lovely,' said the old woman.
'Oh no,' sighed the old man, 'I am not lovely, I wish I were!'
'Your soul is beautiful, my friend,' said the old woman. 'Take this
magic ring, and it will make your face as lovely as your heart.'
She then vanished, and the astonished princess put the flower on
her finger. She immediately became as beautiful as the day,
and many princes asked her hand in marriage. But in the end, she
married one, became queen after her father and had six children.

FAIRY STORY (CORRECT SOLUTION)

Once upon a time there was an ugly princess who lived with her
old father, the king, in a distant land. She was kind and good, but
very sad; she so wanted to be beautiful, and was afraid no
handsome prince would ever love and marry her. One day as she
was walking near the palace, she met an old woman who was
as ugly as she. 'Good morning, my lovely,' said the old woman.
'Oh no,' sighed the princess, 'I am not lovely, I wish I were!'
'Your soul is beautiful, my child,' said the old woman. 'Take this
magic ring, and it will make your face as lovely as your heart.'
She then vanished, and the astonished princess put the ring on her
finger. She immediately became as beautiful as the day, and
many princes asked her hand in marriage. But in the end, she
refused them all, became queen after her father, and ruled the land
well and happily for many years.

Plans for a trip

PLANS FOR A TRIP (MIXED-UP VERSION A)

We are going to take a family of about ten students on a cycling trip to the Himalayas for one week. If you would like to come, please sign your name below. You will need, besides your boats, plenty of light clothing, but also some warm blankets and rainwear; it is usually quite warm at this time of year in our area, but we must be prepared for occasional hotter weather and rain. A small first-aid kit is advisable but not essential as the nurse accompanying us will have a set of medical supplies. Our food will be supplied by the five-star hotels at which we shall be staying; however, you should bring with you two bottles of wine and some compact and nourishing snacks such as dried fruit and Coca Cola. We shall be leaving at 3 a.m. from Victoria Station, London, on 10 July, returning 17 July.

PLANS FOR A TRIP (MIXED-UP VERSION B)

We are going to take a small group of about fifty students on a boating trip to central France for two weeks. If you would like to come, please sign your name below. You will need, besides your bicycles, some heavy walking-shoes, but also warm sweaters and rainwear; it is usually quite warm at this time of year in our area, but we must be prepared for occasional cooler weather and high winds. A small first-aid kit is also necessary as the nurse accompanying us will not have a set of medical supplies. Our food will be supplied by the youth hostels at which we shall be staying; however, you should bring with you two water-bottles and some compact and nourishing snacks such as potato crisps and chocolate. We shall be leaving at 8 a.m. from Victoria Station, London, on 10 December, returning 17 December.

PLANS FOR A TRIP (CORRECT SOLUTION)

We are going to take a small group of about ten students on a cycling trip to central France for one week. If you would like to come, please sign your name below. You will need, besides your bicycles, plenty of light clothing, but also warm sweaters and rainwear; it is usually quite warm at this time of year in our area, but we must be prepared for occasional cooler weather and rain. A small first-aid kit is advisable but not essential as the nurse accompanying us will have a set of medical supplies. Our food will be supplied by the youth hostels at which we shall be staying; however, you should bring with you two water-bottles and some compact and nourishing snacks such as dried fruit and chocolate. We shall be leaving at 8 a.m. from Victoria Station, London, on 10 July, returning 17 July.

Information about a journey

INFORMATION ABOUT A JOURNEY (MIXED-UP VERSION A)

Good morning, ladies and gentlemen. This is your guide speaking. Welcome aboard our biggest airliner, the Duchess 909. The time is 3 p.m. and we have just landed at New York for our non-stop flight westwards to Paris. The sky here is clear, but most of the Indian Ocean, over which we shall be flying, is covered with cloud so we shall not see much of it. The weather in Vienna is at the moment, I regret to say, not very pleasant; there is a blizzard, and the temperature is about the same as in London. However, it may improve by the time we get there. In about half an hour we shall be landing in France. In a short time, I shall give you further details of our height, air-speed and estimated time of arrival. I hope you enjoy your meals. Goodbye.

INFORMATION ABOUT A JOURNEY (MIXED-UP VERSION B)

Hi, ladies and gentlemen! This is your captain, the pilot, speaking. Welcome aboard our biggest ship, the Duchess 909. The time is twelve midnight and we have just taken off from Paris for our non-stop flight westwards to Vienna. The sky here is clear, but most of the Atlantic Ocean, over which we shall be flying, is covered with cloud so we shall not see much of it. The weather in New York is at the moment, I am glad to say, not very exciting; there is a heat-wave, and the temperature is mild. However, it may get worse by the time we get there. In about half an hour we shall be flying over London Bridge. In a short time, I shall give you further details of our height, air-speed and estimated time of take-off. I hope you enjoy your flight. See you.

INFORMATION ABOUT A JOURNEY (MIXED-UP VERSION C)

Good afternoon, ladies and gentlemen. This is the hijacker speaking. Welcome aboard our biggest hovercraft, the Duchess 909. The time is 10 p.m. and we have just crash-landed at London Airport for our non-stop flight westwards to New York. The sky here is clear, but most of the Pacific Ocean, over which we shall be flying, is covered with cloud so we shall not see much of it. The weather in Paris is at the moment, I hope, not too unpleasant; there is a rainstorm, and the temperature is below zero. However, it may not change by the time we get there. In about half an hour we shall be taking off from Ireland. In a short time, I shall give you further details of our height, air-speed and estimated time of meals. I hope you enjoy your holiday. Thank you for your attention.

INFORMATION ABOUT A JOURNEY (CORRECT SOLUTION)

Good afternoon, ladies and gentlemen. This is your captain, the pilot, speaking. Welcome aboard our biggest airliner, the Duchess 909. The time is 3 p.m. and we have just taken off from London Airport for our non-stop flight westwards to New York. The sky here is clear, but most of the Atlantic Ocean, over which we shall be flying, is covered with cloud so we shall not see much of it. The weather in New York is at the moment, I regret to say, not very pleasant; there is a blizzard, and the temperature is below zero. However, it may improve by the time we get there. In about half an hour we shall be flying over Ireland. In a short time, I shall give you further details of our height, air-speed and estimated time of arrival. I hope you enjoy your flight. Thank you for your attention.

In a shop

IN A SHOP (MIXED-UP VERSION A)

Good morning. What a lovely lot of toys you have there. I really must have some. Yes, this is my gun, I always take him shopping with me. I hope you noticed he's pointing straight at you . . . he's so intelligent. Would you mind showing me that money? How much are they? What, only two dollars each? I'm sure you can do better than that. Ah, that's more like it. I'll take the whole set, my boss will be absolutely ecstatic. Please wrap them for me and put it in my suitcase. Thank you so much, you've been very cooperative.

IN A SHOP (MIXED-UP VERSION B)

Good morning. What a beautiful selection of money you have there. I really must have some. Yes, this is my baby, I always take it with me on jobs. Look, it's looking straight at you . . . I'm very accurate. Would you mind giving me those toy cars? How much is there? What, only two hundred dollars? I'm sure you can do better than that. Ah, that's more like it. I'll take the whole cash-box, my baby will find it very useful. Please bring it over here and put them in my bag. Thank you so much, you've been very kind.

IN A SHOP (CORRECT SOLUTION A)

Good morning. What a lovely lot of money you have there. I really must have some. Yes, this is my gun, I always take it with me on jobs. I hope you noticed it's pointing straight at you . . . I'm very accurate. Would you mind giving me that money? How much is there? What, only two hundred dollars? I'm sure you can do better than that. Ah, that's more like it. I'll take the whole cash-box, my boss will find it very useful. Please bring it over here and put it in my suitcase. Thank you so much, you've been very cooperative.

IN A SHOP (CORRECT SOLUTION B)

Good morning. What a beautiful selection of toys you have there. I really must have some. Yes, this is my baby, I always take him shopping with me. Look, he's looking straight at you . . . he's so intelligent. Would you mind showing me those toy cars? How much are they? What, only two dollars each? I'm sure you can do better than that. Ah, that's more like it. I'll take the whole set, my baby will be absolutely ecstatic. Please wrap them up for me and put them in my bag. Thank you so much, you've been very kind.

A letter

A LETTER (MIXED-UP VERSION A)

Dear Mr. Lawrence,

Thank you so much for your letter - you cannot imagine how surprised I was and how distressed. You had been so happy and reserved of late, I was beginning to fear you found our friendship pleasing and wished to end it. But I was completely mistaken; as your letter shows, you want more than friendship.

I am deeply grateful for your dishonourable proposal of marriage, and, subject to my father's consent, would never dream of accepting it.

Yours,

Cecily Underwood.

A LETTER (MIXED-UP VERSION B)

Dear Mr. Lawrence,

Thank you for your letter - you cannot imagine how shocked I was, and how happy. You had been so quiet and affectionate of late, I was sure you found our friendship unsatisfactory and wished to continue it. But I was completely mistaken; as your letter shows, you want more than friendship.

I am deeply offended by your proposal, and, you may be sure, will have the greatest happiness in accepting it.

Yours,

Cecily Underwood.

A LETTER (CORRECT SOLUTION A)

Dear Mr. Lawrence,

Thank you so much for your letter - you cannot imagine how surprised I was and how happy. You had been so quiet and reserved of late, I was beginning to fear you found our friendship unsatisfactory and wished to end it. But I was completely mistaken; as your letter shows, you want more than friendship.

I am deeply grateful for your proposal of marriage, and, subject to my father's consent, will have the greatest happiness in accepting it.

Yours,

Cecily Underwood.

A LETTER (CORRECT SOLUTION B)

Dear Mr. Lawrence,

Thank you for your letter - you cannot imagine how shocked I was and how distressed. You had been so happy and affectionate of late, I was sure you found our friendship pleasing and wished to continue it. But I was completely mistaken; as your letter shows, you want more than friendship.

I am deeply offended by your dishonourable proposal, and, you may be sure, would never dream of accepting it.

Yours,

Cecily Underwood.

Compound activities

These combine elements of both brainstorming and organizing activities; this does not necessarily mean that they are composed of several stages (though they may be), or that they are more complex. On the whole, however, they are relatively time-consuming, and entail a wide variety of thinking processes (both logical and imaginative) and language functions. They are therefore appropriate for more adult and advanced students. Even native speakers may find them interesting to do.

13   Composing letters

The task here is to compose appropriate responses to letters that are in some way provocative: advising, insulting, appealing, complaining, threatening – anything, in fact, which stimulates a reaction from the recipient. The content of such 'stimulus' letters is based on 'human interest' situations of dilemma or conflict, such as misunderstandings or quarrels between lovers, family complications, work problems, and so on; they thus provide an excellent foundation on which to build discussions about such subjects.

Such letters are not hard to prepare: a few varied examples are given at the end of this section, but teachers may like to compose their own, using problems familiar to their students. Enough copies of the letters should be duplicated so that every participant, or at least every two, can have one.

No specific set of language items needs preparation here: the language used depends completely on the type of letter. However, teachers may wish to use this opportunity to teach or revise the conventions of letter-writing: the headings, openings and endings appropriate to different levels of formality. These levels of formality are expressed too in the type of language used in the body of the letters, and this is another point which may need teaching: the structures and vocabulary suitable for an informal, chatty letter such as (f) are totally different from those used in a formal note like (h). Students should be reminded that they should, on the whole, reply to letters at the same level of formality as that in which they were written.

The organization of this exercise is very simple: the teacher explains the task, distributes copies of the stimulus letter and (optionally) goes over the text to clarify any difficult language; she then divides the class into groups, who read (or reread) the letter, choose one of their number to be 'secretary', and begin to discuss the composition of their reply. In the feedback, each group reads out its answer; participants will enjoy hearing their own compositions and will be interested in the different reactions of other groups. It is possible to go further: compare the different responses, and discuss their relative merits. A variation is to take *two* letters, purporting to be from two people involved in the situation and embodying totally different viewpoints; some groups are then given one such letter and the rest are given the other – see examples (a) and (b), (c) and (d), (e) and (f). In the feedback session this time, the stimulus letters will have to be read out as well as the answers (unless the teacher has already done so before the discussion). In either case, if the results are good and interesting enough, students may be asked to copy them out neatly to be displayed on the wall of the classroom, together with the letters they have answered; this provides both encouragement and an opportunity for all students to reread their groups' compositions and review the language used.

Where letters are obviously aimed at a single individual, for example, (g) and (h), there is not much scope for group role-play. However, this is not true of situations where replies could conceivably be composed by several people together: letters addressed to agony columns of women's magazines – (a), (b) and (f) – can be answered by the 'editorial committee' of the column; the headmaster addressed in letters (c) and (d) could call a 'staff meeting' to help him compose suitable replies; letter (j) could be discussed by all the 'family'; and so on.

The first six of the following examples are divided into pairs for use in the variation described above; but they may equally well be used separately. Examples (a) and (b) are adaptations of the letters whose composition I described on p. 12.

a) Dear Helpful Harriet,
    I don't know what to do about my mother. She is always criticizing me—the way I dress, the way I speak or look . . . I can't even read a book without her interrupting me to ask what it's about and telling me whether I should be reading it or not, and why! And of course, every moment of my time away from her has to

be accounted for (by me) and commented on (by her).

I try to tell her to stop interfering with my life, but it doesn't seem to help; and I've nobody to advise me—my father is dead, and I am an only child.

It's not as if my mother has any worries; we're fairly well off, and she doesn't have to work, only do the housekeeping. I've now met a wonderful girl who I want to take out, but I'm afraid to bring her to the house—when she meets my mother, she won't want to know me any more. I am nineteen.

Please help me!

Fed up Son.

b) Dear Helpful Harriet,

What am I to do about my nineteen-year-old son, my only child? He means so much to me, especially since his father died, and I have always tried to give him all I could. He has never wanted for anything money could buy, and I have given him all my love and attention. But nowadays he meets all my affectionate inquiries with curt retorts, or even tells me to mind my own business. I try not to show him how hurt I am by his attitude, but often I just go off and cry. Sometimes I even feel he hates me, while I do my best to show him how much I love him and care about everything he does.

I have given him so much: is this my reward?

Hurt Mother

c) Dear Headmaster,

I am writing to complain about the treatment my eight-year-old child has received at your school. A talented, original child, used to being given plenty of attention and play material, I find he has been forced to sit at a desk, immobile for hours on end, copying letters and numbers and being made to read boring words when he would much rather be occupied in a creative activity such as painting or drama. When he in fact stopped doing these boring exercises on his own initiative and went into a corner to draw, he was scolded and punished, but surely his action was only natural? His attempts to explain why

he did not wish to do the routine exercises were treated as
rudeness and suppressed; is this how you stimulate creative
self-expression? He has, moreover, received little individual
attention from his teacher. Used to being the focus of constant
affectionate attention at his kindergarten, he is now scarcely
noticed; the teacher, he says, sometimes does not speak to him
personally even once in the course of a whole lesson!

I hope you will look into the matter and take appropriate
action.

Yours truly
(Mrs) Yvonne Boddington-Smith

d)   Memorandum

To: The Headmaster
From: Jane Brown, Class 3b
Subject: Cecil Boddington-Smith

This child is new this term and is very difficult. Having
been kept at private kindergarten until he was seven, he is
very behind in the elementary skills of reading, writing and
arithmetic, and has no notion of classroom discipline. I have
tried to assist his progress by giving him individual work-cards
he can do while the others are working on more advanced material;
but he does not concentrate, and has even on occasion left his
desk, without permission, to take up unprofitable occupations
such as playing and drawing. When I have remonstrated with him,
he has reacted with sullenness or impertinence.

His progress has naturally been very slow (though I am
convinced he is a bright child), and his behaviour is having a
bad effect on the whole class. The latter is composed of
thirty-six eight-year-olds from varying backgrounds; it is far
from easy to control and teach such a group to the standard
required by this school; and added disruptive influences such
as this child make it near impossible.

e) My dear Mary,

I have been up all night in mental agony trying to think what to do, and I have decided to appeal to you once again. What have I done to deserve such treatment? We have spent such wonderful times together - parties, theatres, picnics - which I thought you enjoyed as much as I did. I have not tried to impose on you, I have always been polite and considerate, and I thought you loved me as much as I love you, though you never said so. Then suddenly last week you refused one of my invitations, your mother will not let me speak to you on the phone, and if I call at your house, you are 'not in'. What has happened? What have I done?

My last letter was returned with a brief note saying you no longer wished to see me, but how can you treat me like this? Surely I merit some sort of explanation? I cannot stop loving you as if I were switching off a light. Please answer this.

Your ever-loving

John.

f) Dear Helpful Harriet,

What am I to do with an ex-boyfriend who won't leave me alone? We had quite a good time together while it lasted, he was always taking me out to classy restaurants and expensive shows, but he was so serious! Always talking about love, mutual empathy, soul-mates and stuff like that. I'm sure I never gave him cause to think I wanted to marry him or anything. Anyhow, I got fed up in the end and started dropping hints like 'Why don't you take out some other girls?', or made excuses not to go out. But he wouldn't catch on, so I just refused to see him any more, and got my family to help keep him away. Now I keep getting these sentimental letters which I don't answer, but it's getting me down. He just won't take 'no' for an answer. What should I do?

Mary

g) Dear Jack,

You will find this note when you get back from the office today. I'm leaving you, at least for the time being, perhaps for good, and going to live with Mother. I don't suppose you even noticed how miserable I've been since the children left home. I'm just the woman who cooks your meals and does your laundry, you never <u>talk</u> to me, do you? And when was the last time you took me out? There's no point going on complaining, you'll only say it's because you've got no time, you're too busy with that new job you got promoted to, and your classy friends. Well, now I'm gone you can find yourself a posh upper-class wife to go with them, much better than me, even if I have been married to you for twenty years.

Sheila

h) Dear Mr Jones,

You have been an employee of our company for some years now, and I have never before found any reason to complain of your conduct. However, a matter has come to my notice which I feel cannot be ignored.

Your colleague, Miss Thorpe, came to me in great distress saying she had seen you betting large sums of money in the local casino, when you were obviously the worse for drink. I have no reason to doubt the veracity of Miss Thorpe's statement. This company has always prided itself on the integrity and proper behaviour of its employees; drinking and gambling are quite intolerable. It seems to me also a suspicious circumstance that you should have had in your possession the amount of money described by Miss Thorpe; our salary would certainly not afford you such sums.·

I must request your immediate resignation.

Yours truly,

Maurice Brand
(Manager)

i) Dear Dr. Elliot,

I have been advised to write to you for advice; I understand you are an expert on the care of brain-damaged children and their families.

I have four children, of whom the youngest, Carol, is severely spastic. We all love her very much and have cared for her for the first four years of her life. She is now, however, getting difficult to look after: she cannot walk and is heavy to carry; dressing, feeding and bathing her take most of my time, and I cannot help feeling I am neglecting the other children, aged eight, twelve and fourteen. I never seem to have time to talk to them or look after them properly and they all (the older ones particularly) spend more and more time outside the house.

My husband and I are considering putting Carol in a home. We should hate to do this, as we love her very much, but wonder if it might not be fairer to the rest of the family.

I should be very grateful for your advice.

Yours sincerely,
Monica Standish

j) **Dear Mr Hunter**

Thank you for your letter of 15 June, in which you refused our offer of a post in our Canadian offices. We should nevertheless very much like you to reconsider.

The post offers you a substantial increase in salary, and opportunities for further promotion, neither of which you can hope for in your present situation. We understand that your wife is against the move, and that your two younger children have

health problems; but we hope very much that these
are difficulties that can be overcome. As for
your eldest son's place at University, we can
assure you that Canadian education is by no means
inferior to that available in this country.

We feel that you are the most suitable
candidate for the post, and are sure you would find
the work satisfying and rewarding.

Yours very sincerely,

James Charon
(Personnel Manager)

14 Debates

In Part 1, I discussed the limitations and disadvantages of the
conventional class debate as a vehicle for fluency practice
(pp. 5–6): the limited scope of its subjects (social, political or
philosophical controversies), and the relative lack of participation
(since it has to be a full-class, not a small-group activity). It would
be a pity, however, to exclude the debate completely from our
battery of communication exercises; many students (particularly
the more adult and intellectual) enjoy this kind of discussion;
and the skills of oratory and dialectics are learned and exercised in
a debate better than anywhere else. Perhaps its disadvantages
may be mitigated and its advantages preserved by using the
following procedure.

The class is divided into two or three groups, each of whom is
given a motion for debate: two of these are the direct opposite
of each other (for example, 'Marriage is a perfect institution' and
'Marriage should be abolished'); and a third – optional – a
compromise ('Marriage laws need reforming'). Alternatively,
there may be four to six different motions, each one supporting a
different point of view; then, of course, the class will be divided
into the corresponding number of groups. In the 'balloon' debate,
for example, four to six famous people are imagined to be
hanging in a basket suspended from a balloon which is gradually
deflating; one after another they will have to be thrown out to
keep the balloon airborne, and ultimately only one will survive;

the debate has to decide which person is most worth preserving. Other such sets of 'competitive' subjects to be discussed and voted on are given in examples (n) to (r).

In any case, whether there are two, three or several groups, the first stage in the activity is the same: each group has to work out and note down all possible arguments in favour of its motion (or candidate, in the 'balloon' debate), including defences against points that might be brought up by the opposition. It also has to work out the presentation of this material (who will put which argument and how), using every member of the group.

The groups can be divided according to the actual opinions of the students; but I have usually found it more effective to divide them arbitrarily, so that many will find themselves having to argue in favour of something they oppose, or vice-versa. This is in fact a kind of role-play, and works very well as a rule; it also has the positive side-effect of making participants consider seriously the justifications behind other people's points of view. However, where students are deeply committed or feel very strongly about some issue, they may resent being asked to argue against it, and should not be asked to do so; teachers will probably be aware which subjects are likely to provoke such a reaction. In any case, it is not a good idea to choose a topic which excites violent opposition or defence; such excitement makes for disorganized debating and excessive use of the native language.

A time-limit should be set for the groups to prepare their cases – ten to fifteen minutes is usually enough – then students rearrange their seating to suit a full class discussion: in a circle, for example, or even in the conventional rows.

The degree of formality of the debate depends on the teacher and on what her class is used to: she may wish to adopt the traditions of formal 'parliamentary' procedure, or she may prefer a looser, less rigid structure, with only a chairman to regulate participation. If a proposer and seconder are going to be needed, then of course students should have been told this before their group preparation; other formalities of procedure can be outlined by the teacher before the full debate begins. These should include such points as: what the chairman does, how participants indicate they want to speak, how long they may do so, how far interruptions are to be tolerated, and so on.

The full debate then ensues. It is to be hoped that all will participate, since each student will have been allotted a part of the 'case' to put across, and the preparatory discussions supply both, or all, sides with plenty of ready 'ammunition' for their speeches. Where students were originally divided into groups arbitrarily (not according to their real opinions), the teacher must use her own discretion as to whether they have to continue to support their group's motion during the entire debate, or whether they may be allowed to express their own views; it depends how far the debate is seen on the one hand as a game-like activity, and on the other as a serious argument. In either case, the final voting should be 'genuine' (otherwise there is little point in it!); the announcement of the results of the vote constitutes the end of the activity.

Some examples of motions are given below. Examples (a) to (i) are for-and-against types, in which the opposing motion is actually written out as a counter-proposal implying a contradiction of the first; I have found this offers more stimulation for discussion, but it is optional: groups can simply be asked to support or oppose one proposition. The compromise suggestion which appears as the third proposition in examples (j) to (m) is also optional. Examples (n) to (r) are for use in the multiple-choice type of debate, such as the 'balloon' debate described above.

a) Love your country.
   Patriotism is outdated.

b) Everyone should be equal.
   Equality is neither possible nor desirable.

c) Children are little savages, tamed by the environment.
   Children are basically innocent and good, spoiled only by their environment.

d) Prisons should be abolished.
   More prisons should be built.

e) Nature gives us the best things in life.
   Civilization saves us from the cruelty of nature.

f) Riches make for happiness.
   Money can't make you happy.

g) Religion is the opium of the masses.
   Religion is the greatest force for moral good.

h) With age comes wisdom.
   Older is not necessarily wiser.

i) We learn through our mistakes.
   We learn by doing things right.

j) Marriage is a perfect institution.
   Marriage should be abolished.
   Marriage laws need reforming.

k) The possession of marijuana should be illegal.
Marijuana should be completely legalized.
There should be some control over drug traffic.

l) A woman's place is in the home.
A woman's place is no more in the home than a man's is.
Feminists will have to compromise over the woman's role in the family.

m) There is no excuse for using corporal punishment in schools.
Spare the rod and spoil the child.
Corporal punishment should be used only as a last resort.

n) (for a 'balloon' debate) The person most worth preserving from death is: a politician/a sportsman/a writer/a television personality/a scientist. (The teacher will, of course, use named personalities here, suitable to the cultural background of the students.)

o) The best place to live is: a flat/a caravan/a castle/a cottage/a tent.

p) The best hobby to have is: stamp-collecting/hiking/theatre-going/carpentry.

q) The most worthwhile subject to study is: English/science/history/literature/psychology.

r) The best profession to have is: policeman/explorer/teacher/politician/nurse.

15 Publicity campaigns

Theoretical arguments such as those used in debating have no place in this next exercise which is a thoroughly down-to-earth kind of project. The task is to plan a publicity campaign, consisting of a series of measures whose objective is to convince the public of something: that they should vote for a certain politician, that they should come to a particular entertainment, exhibition or celebration, that they should have less children (see the end of this section for a fuller list of such 'causes').

Apart from choosing a subject and thinking a little how *she* would tackle it, the teacher has virtually nothing to prepare for this activity. Nor are there any particular structures or lexical items which need revising with the students. However, publicity campaigns use some very specific varieties of language, and the teacher might like to take advantage of this opportunity to discuss them: I am referring in particular to the use of language in the

mass media, especially where its aim is to make a swift impact on
the reader or hearer – newspaper headlines, slogans, advertising
jargon, 'commercial' jingles, and so on. It might be a good idea to
bring examples of these to the classroom and talk about the
differences between such 'impact' language and ordinary
conversation. This knowledge can then be implemented in the
execution of the task.

After a preliminary explanation of the assignment before them,
students are presented with their subjects, told what audience their
campaigns are to be aimed at, and divided into groups. It is
possible to give everyone the same subject; but I have found it
better to give three or four alternatives and let each group choose
what they want: some topics just do not seem to attract, and it
is difficult to tell in advance which. Participants are asked first to
brainstorm all sorts of measures that might be taken to publicize
their cause, with no limit of budget or facilities. For those who
have difficulty getting started, the teacher might suggest a few of
the following ideas: television programmes, radio interviews,
lectures, newspaper articles, leaflets, slogans, posters, films,
rallies, demonstrations, advertisements, 'happenings'.

After ten or fifteen minutes the teacher can stop the talking and
have an interim feedback session: each group is invited to
describe one or two of its most attractive ideas (not all of them – it
takes too long!). This gives the teacher an opportunity to help
groups along by encouragement and constructive criticism ('Yes,
a demonstration is a good idea, but have you thought how you
are going to get people to come?' 'Mobile loudspeakers? Yes, they
certainly attract attention, but some people might be disturbed
and annoyed – better think carefully about time and place . . .'). It
also allows for some useful 'cross-fertilization' between groups.

After this, the groups begin planning their campaigns in detail.
Of what, exactly, will the television programme consist? What
will they put in the newspaper article? What will the slogans be,
and how will they be publicized? In other words, without actually
composing the precise content of the longer items, detailed briefs
should be made up for every measure suggested. A supply of
pencils and rough paper is essential here! Time-schedules
and limitations of budget can be laid down at this stage, decided
by the teacher or by the students themselves.

Role-play can be introduced at any stage: the group may be a
town council, a political party executive, a conservationist
pressure group, a student council, a government commission, or
any body which seems appropriate to the subject of the campaign.
Within this body, each student may have a specific role.
Organizational roles include the chairman (concerned with efficient

process), the secretary (concerned with clarifying and recording ideas), and the treasurer (who wants to keep down expenses). *Socio-economic roles* include the mother, the poor man, the student, the teacher, the farmer, the entertainer, the businessman, the policeman, the doctor. *Character roles* may include people who are sceptical, enthusiastic, quick-tempered, over-critical, impatient, bossy, pessimistic, optimistic, intolerant, yes-men, sticklers for detail, lazy, stingy, conservative. Such roles may be distributed in combinations: for example, a student may be told he is to be the secretary, who is also a rather irritable local shopkeeper.

When plans of campaign have been worked out in a fair amount of detail, the teacher may feel that enough has been done, and begin to draw the activity to a close. In this case, groups should be given the opportunity to display their results, but detailed description by each can be tedious: the ideas can be written out or sketched by the students and put up on the wall; or the teacher can take in what has been done and herself describe briefly the highlights of each campaign to the whole class.

However, if it is wished, the activity can overflow into succeeding lessons, and students be asked to actually execute some or all of their ideas: to design their posters, role-play and record their interviews, paint their slogans on billboards or banners, write their articles. Finally, the resulting material is displayed on the walls of the classroom or, where appropriate, delivered orally.

Here are some possible subjects:

- Make our roads safe!
- X for President/Mayor/Student representative!
- Help the police!
- Raise wages!
- Keep our countryside/town clean!
- Stop inflation!
- Stop cruelty to animals/children!
- Free the exploited worker/woman/child!
- Abolish exams!
- Stop pollution!
- Join our Youth club/Dramatic society/Group!
- Have less babies!
- Come to our festival/carnival/fair/sale!
- Help our charity!
- Come to live in our country!

16 Surveys

Most students are familiar with opinion polls or surveys. They are
easily adapted for use in this type of discussion. In order for this
to be done in the classroom, the sources of information or the
population samples to be taken are limited to the actual members
of the class.

Each group is given a general heading indicating the area of
information required (examples below). As a first stage, they are
required to brainstorm the particular subjects they will want to
investigate. For example, if the subject is television viewing, they
might want to find out how much time people spend viewing,
what their favourite programmes are, what they think of
particular types of broadcast, how they think television could be
improved.

Next, the groups have to decide how the questions will be put.
There are three main possibilities: the open-ended type ('What
do you think of programme X?'); the agree/disagree type ('Is
programme X a waste of time? Yes/No'); and the multiple-
choice ('Programme X is exciting/interesting/not very
interesting/boring'). The advantage of the first is that it gives the
answerer more latitude to express his exact opinion; but on the
other hand a large number of very varied answers are difficult to
assess and express as a general statistical conclusion. The
second and third types give rather crude approximations of
answerers' views, but they are relatively quick and easy to fill in
and score.

Thirdly, the questions have to be formulated and written down.
The teacher may find it a good idea to limit the number of such
questions (to, say, ten); then quicker groups can be allowed to
append extra ones while the others are finishing. It is surprisingly
difficult to formulate questions that are clear, unambiguous,
relevant, objective, and whose answers will in fact supply the
information the inquirers want. The teacher may need to point
out irrelevancies, ambiguities etc., and generally help students to
be critical of their own efforts: a good deal of time should be spent
talking about suggested questions, picking holes in them and
improving them.

Fourthly, the questionnaire has actually to be administered.
This can be done within the group, with the same students both
asking and answering the questions. But it is perhaps more
interesting all round to try them out on someone else. For this,
there must be an even number of groups. At a given moment,
even if not all the questionnaires are completely drafted, all groups
stop preparing them. Then half the groups start interviewing the

other half; when they have finished, they change over so that those who were answering have a chance to interrogate others.

For the final stages, the groups reconvene separately, compute their results, agree upon the conclusions, and make known their findings to the class as a whole, in the form of a brief oral or written report.

This time role-play is not appropriate, as much of the interest comes from the natural curiosity of students to know the authentic results of such surveys. Here are some subjects:

– Television viewing: habits, or opinions on programmes
– Family backgrounds
– Attitudes to school/university/job
– Spending habits
– Leisure-time occupation
– Political views
– Attitudes to different academic subjects or teachers
– Ideas about child-rearing
– Eating habits
– Attitudes to controversial subjects such as those suggested on
  pp. 107–8.

17 Planning projects

This is the last activity in the book, and perhaps the most ambitious: it combines elements from many of the other exercises, may run into several sessions, and is suitable for mature, advanced students. Groups are set the task of planning in detail some sort of socio-economic enterprise, four examples of which are described below: a commune, an educational institution, a business and an expedition. A wide range of aspects needs to be considered in such planning: problems of authority and administration, individual needs, social relations, economic viability, and many more. The discussions are therefore correspondingly long and complex, but also very absorbing and involving.

Classes can be introduced to their task in a number of different ways. They can simply be told that they have to start planning the project not by playing a specified role but as themselves; in this case, the teacher's instructions might run: 'If tomorrow someone in authority were to come to you and say "you've got to set up this project", how would you do it?'. Another option is to give students a defined imaginary situation and some limitations to go with it: 'You are a band of pioneers who have just set foot on an uninhabited but fertile island and want to set up an ideal community there; the year is 1700.' Or one can go even further and give each student an individual role (some examples are given in the sections below). Prescribed roles, whether group or individual, should be written on cards or slips of paper and distributed to students for reference. However, role-play may be employed without the use of role-cards: the groups can be given no background information about themselves, but asked as the first stage in the task to decide who and where they are, and when the whole thing is taking place. After this, each participant can invent and give some information about his individual role within the imagined group: 'I am the Captain of the ship that brought us here' . . . 'I am the Captain's wife, we have five children.' One condition of this is that once a student has established any details of his role, these may not be contradicted by anyone else: for example, a participant role-playing the son of the Captain and his wife may not claim to be an only child!

Once these preliminaries have been sorted out, the main task may be tackled. Because it is so complex, some organizational measures need to be taken in order to break it down into manageable stages. It may be a good idea, for instance, to start with a full class brainstorming session in which students suggest what seem to them to be the major problems to be faced when planning their project. The teacher can, of course, prepare information sheets to guide discussions with such points ready listed; but on the whole it is better if these are suggested by the students themselves; the teacher can always supplement if necessary. The sort of ideas which will be thrown out will be expressed mostly as questions, and can be noted briefly on the blackboard or overhead projector; for example: *'Who'll do what?'* *'How will we support ourselves?'* Fuller suggested lists of such problems are given below for each project separately.

These brainstormed suggestions give the groups some preliminary direction of thought, but the whole subject is still rather complex and unwieldy. Before tackling it in their group discussions, therefore, students should be encouraged to plan the *process* of their negotiations carefully. They should consider at least the following questions: Do all the (brainstormed) questions need discussing? Can they be whittled down? Or do some even need dividing into separate topics? In what order should they be dealt with? Can some be discussed simultaneously by sub-groups? Once the group knows exactly what aspects they are going to discuss, in what order, and how, they can with confidence embark on detailed planning.

Decisions should be carefully noted as they are made, as they form the basis for the next stage, which is the preparation of a 'blueprint' for the projected enterprise. This can be done in the form of brief but clear notes, or expanded into a full essay, with appended sketches, diagrams and maps where relevant.

If the feedback session is to take the form of verbal descriptions of results, then groups should be directed to spend a short time preparing them, after they have finished their plans: deciding who will say what, which diagrams or sketches will need putting up on the blackboard or overhead projector and who will draw them, in what order different aspects will be described, and so on. Such lectures may be a little time-consuming, but the length of the feedback should be in proportion to the time spent on the rest of the exercise; and the detailed preparation will help to tighten up delivery. A shorter alternative is simply to put up the 'blueprints' on the classroom wall as a display for all to read and admire!

All this takes some time: at the very least the full activity should take an hour and a half, and it can run to two or three times as much. If it is wished, the subject can be dealt with even more thoroughly and the problems investigated more deeply and seriously by adding an element of study: the teacher may introduce articles, pictures, film-strips and books about the type of project under discussion; or she may invite someone who has experience in a real similar enterprise to give a talk and answer questions.

Communes

Various attempts have been made, particularly in the twentieth century, to set up communes or other ideal communities, and here the students are invited to consider how they would go about doing so themselves.

If the groups are given no fixed setting, then the first thing they will need to decide is the general socio-political direction their commune will take: will it be idealistically socialist? Or aim for maximum freedom of the individual? Will its government be democratic, or authoritarian? Will it be selective in any way?

Then an agenda has to be prepared. Some points which should be included: means of subsistence, division of labour, division of rewards, decision-making and administration, main laws, child care and education, geographical layout, cultural and religious activity.

For this project (which is the most comprehensive and intricate of the four) it is best to let students choose their own roles, as described above, within the group situation, three examples of which are given below. These settings are only suggestions: teachers may wish to adapt them to suit their own students' cultural background, or give no setting at all and let participants invent their own.

a) You are a conservationist back-to-nature group of families with children, leaving town to set up an ideal community in the country. You have very little capital – enough, perhaps, to build one six-room house. You aim to be entirely self-sufficient, but realize you may have to compromise at first.

b) You are a group of left-wing revolutionaries who are trying to overthrow a despotic regime. Forced to flee the city, you are setting up camp in the mountains. You have no children with you, but two of your women are pregnant. You realize you may have to be in this camp for some years and are determined to make a pleasant and viable home of it. You have a little financial assistance from sympathizers abroad – enough to cover the bare essentials of life.

c) You are pioneers, some single and some married, who have arrived in a new, hitherto unexplored region: a large, uninhabited island, rich in water, vegetation and wild life. You wish to set up a new home which will make for the maximum happiness of all. Some of you are religious, some not. You have no contact with the outside world (your ship sank). The year is 1700.

Educational institutions

The idea of setting up a school, college or university is closer to home and altogether simpler. The new institution can be based on that which the students are at present attending. They usually have strong convictions about what needs change and reform; here is their chance to express their criticisms in a constructive and imaginative way: if they had the job of rebuilding and replanning the whole institution, how would they do it? Alternatively they may be asked to plan for another totally imaginary situation; three suggestions are given below.

Points to be considered should include: finance, size and scope, type of students, staffing, range of subjects offered, facilities, geographical position and layout, organization and administration, extra-curricular activities, rules. Here are some possible group and individual roles:

a) You are a committee appointed to set up a new university in a town of twenty thousand inhabitants. You have a generous budget which will enable you to build and equip an entire campus. The surrounding area is heavily industrialized, and up to now a relatively low proportion of the population has gone on to further education; it is hoped that the existence of a local university may change this.

Roles: an architect, a town councillor, a prospective student, his father/mother, an influential local businessman, experienced teachers and administrators.

b) A high school is to be built in a suburb of the capital city of this country/state; up to now the children have attended a big school half an hour's journey away. The local population is mainly middle class and well off, most of the parents being university graduates. The school will provide for about three hundred children between the ages of fourteen and eighteen. The money available will cover basic buildings and equipment, but will not run to luxuries (what are 'luxury' and what are 'basic' items will depend on national standards!)

Roles: as in (a) above.

c) You are a committee appointed to set up a primary school in a remote village in tropical Africa, where no school has existed before, for about sixty children ranging in age from eight to fourteen. You have three trained teachers and three or four young people from the village who have finished their high school education and are willing to help. You have no buildings, enough money for only the crudest equipment, and will have to improvise.

Roles:
– The head teacher, dedicated and enthusiastic, but perhaps over-ambitious.
– An older teacher of some experience, wise, but rather sceptical and defeatist.
– A young teacher fresh from university, town-bred and out of touch with local conditions.
– The head-man, eager for his village to have the school, willing to help, but doesn't want to offend villagers.
– A villager, father of prospective pupils, suspicious of innovations, would rather things stayed as they are.
– A young woman from the village, uneducated but eager to be involved.

Businesses

For adults with some knowledge and experience in making a living, it might be interesting to set up a business with certain given resources – say, a specific sum of money. Such businesses can range from money-making speculations to philanthropic charities; some suggestions are given below. There is no intrinsic reason why the firms should be legal: it might appeal to some students' sense of humour to try to set up illegal rackets, as in the last four examples. In any case, issues to be dealt with should include: exact scope of activity, raising (additional) capital, premises, personnel, marketing, advertising, a name. Here are some possible businesses:

– a shop
– a private investigator's bureau
– a theatre
– a children's summer camp
– a charity
– a new magazine
– an assassination bureau
– a smuggling agency
– a kidnapping organization
– a blackmailing organization

The roles needed for this exercise should be defined in terms of talents, abilities and experience rather than personality. Here are seven that might be used:

– A middle-aged man with some business experience and a little capital, but no particular talents.
– An artist of some ability, specializing in graphics, but unable to make a living by freelance work.
– A brilliant mathematician just out of university with no job.
– A writer, has published a novel or two, but wants a part-time job that would use his talents.
– A garage mechanic of some experience, has a 'knack' with machines, very hard worker and reliable.
– A middle-aged woman who has been a housewife for many years; her children now grown up, she wants a job.
– An out-of-work science teacher, fed up with teaching, wants to make some money.

To these, of course, may be added further personality traits according to the imagination of the students.

Expeditions

How would students like to set off on an expedition to the Amazon Basin or to the South Pole? An uncomfortable, perhaps, but exciting idea that needs plenty of planning and organization.

117

Students may be given a destination and purpose, as in the examples below, or they may be asked, as the first stage in their discussions, to decide alone where they are going and why. Similarly, roles may be allotted or the students choose their own; or the activity may be done without role-play at all.

Groups will need to discuss these points: destination and aim (if not prescribed), distribution of responsibility, financing (will they need a sponsor? if so, how will they find one?), equipment and supplies, route and time-schedule, communications, methods of work at their destination, recording and publication of results. Here are some expeditions:

- The Amazonian jungle, to study wild life.
- North Africa, to study Beduin customs.
- New Guinea, to study local dialects.
- The Andes, to map a previously unmapped area.
- The Himalayas, to climb a mountain.
- India, to follow the Ganges river from source to sea.
- Round the world for fun.
- American black ghettoes, to study race relations.
- Australian outback, to simulate and study aboriginal life-style.
- Indonesia, to collect animals for a zoo.

Roles, if prescribed, should have defined characteristics of personality and temperament as well as ability and experience: part of the planning will depend on who is likely to get on with whom, and how people may react in difficult physical and psychological situations. Here are some possibilities:

- A doctor, aged forty, has been on two or three such expeditions before, unmarried, a quiet phlegmatic type.
- Young sailor, rich, owns his own yacht and has sailed round the world in it. Brave and strong, a bit quick-tempered.
- Young lady, married to the sailor, also likes sailing, no experience, but enthusiastic and charming, willing to try her hand at anything.
- Nurse, aged thirty-five, divorced, very good references from her hospital, wants a break from routine. Rather cold personality, but reliable.
- Explorer, veteran of many such expeditions, aged sixty, healthy, very knowledgeable, rather bossy.
- Naturalist, aged forty-five, has done a lot of field-work, written books, and is well-known. Pleasant and popular, but diabetic.
- Naturalist's wife, aged forty-four, devoted to husband, excellent cook and housewife, amiable, but tense and over-anxious.

Bibliography

More practical ideas

There are a large number of books on the subject of classroom discussions in a foreign language. Most of them, however, 'feed' the students with too much of both language and content of the projected discussions, and provide no further motivation to talk: the resulting conversation is often not very enjoyable or effective. Some notable exceptions:

Alan Maley and Alan Duff, *Drama techniques in language learning*, Cambridge University Press, 1978.
Many excellent ideas, largely based on classroom experience. Differs from *Discussions that work* in that the talking is stimulated by a developing dramatic situation rather than by a pre-set task.
Andrew Wright, Michael Buckby, Michael Betteridge, *Games for language learning*, Cambridge University Press, 1979.
A very practical handbook, full of good, clearly described 'talking' games. Many of these are more suitable for younger learners, but can be adapted for adults and more advanced work.
Susan Holden (ed.), *Visual aids for classroom interaction*, Modern English Publications, 1978.
Imaginative but practical ideas for using visual aids to get students talking, suggested by a number of experienced teachers and materials-writers. The activities are on the whole short and simple; some demand a fair amount of preparation.
M. M. Webster and E. W. Castanon, *Crosstalk*, Oxford University Press, 1980.
A set of three books with lots of attractively set-out ideas for discussion-games. Again, perhaps a little too much is put into the students' mouths in advance but there is plenty of excellent material to use as it is or to adapt.
Christine Frank, Mario Rinvolucri, Margaret Berer, *Challenge to think*, Oxford University Press, 1981.
A book of puzzles and problems to be solved by group interaction.
Alan Maley, Françoise Grellet, *Mind Matters*, Cambridge University Press, 1981.
A book of games, puzzles and problem-solving activities for class use.
Susan Holden (ed.), *Modern English Teacher*, Modern English Publications.
Not a book but a periodical of practical suggestions for language-learning activities. Its contributors are nearly all practising teachers, and their suggestions are therefore based on classroom experience. Good ideas for discussions can be found in most issues.

Materials for specific activities

Texts

Different kinds of texts to be used in activities such as *Combining versions* and *Sentence-sequence* can be found in the following books.

Michael Swan, *Spectrum* and *Kaleidoscope,* Cambridge University Press, 1978.
Alan Maley and Alan Duff, *Words!,* Cambridge University Press, 1976.
Alan Duff, *That's life,* Cambridge University Press, 1979.
Susan Morris, *Love,* Cambridge University Press, 1980.
  These five books are treasuries of 'bits' of written texts of every kind: jokes, advertisements, articles, rhymes, letters etc.
Geoffrey Summerfield (ed.), *Voices* and *Junior Voices,* Penguin books, 1968 and 1970.
  Excellent anthologies of verse, mostly modern; not too difficult for our students, but nevertheless 'real' poetry.
Alan Maley and Alan Duff, *Variations on a theme,* Cambridge University Press, 1978.
  A series of short dialogues, open to interpretation by reader or listener.

Controversial issues

The following books give a variety of subjects to be argued about, which can be used in *Making a case, Composing letters* or *Surveys.*

Michael Ockenden, *Talking points,* Longman, 1977.
  Mostly personal, social or moral dilemmas.
L. G. Alexander, R. H. Kingsbury, *I think, you think,* Longman, 1977.
L. G. Alexander, R. H. Kingsbury, John Chapman, *Take a stand,* Longman, 1978. (American English equivalent to *I think, you think.*)
L. G. Alexander, Monica C. Vincent, *Make your point,* Longman, 1975.
L. G. Alexander, Monica C. Vincent, John Chapman, *Talk it over,* Longman, 1978. (American English equivalent to *Make your point.*)
  Mostly contemporary political or social issues. *I think you think* and *Take a stand* are more suitable for adults, *Make your point* and *Talk it over* for adolescents.

Pictures

For use in various activities: *Interpreting pictures, Finding connections, Picture differences,* and several others.

Paul Groves, Nigel Grimshaw, *The Goodbodys,* Edward Arnold, 1976.
L. A. Hill, *Picture Composition Book,* Longman, 1960.
J. B. Heaton, *Composition through pictures,* Longman, 1960.
  These are all books of strip-cartoons or series of pictures that make up stories, to be used singly or in (or out of) sequence. (An additional excellent source of strip-cartoons is your local newspaper.)
Donn Byrne and Andrew Wright, *What do you think?,* Longman, 1974.
  A selection of photographs and drawings to be used as a basis for oral activities.

Alan Maley, Alan Duff, Françoise Grellet, *The Mind's Eye,* Cambridge
University Press, 1980.
Excellent collections of clear pictures, cartoons, designs etc., for use in
the foreign language classroom. These can be used as bases for
discussions suggested in this book, or according to directions given by
the authors.

Recorded sounds

Alan Maley and Alan Duff, *Sounds Interesting* and *Sounds Intriguing,*
Cambridge University Press, 1975 and 1979.
Taped sequences of unexplained sounds on cassette to be used in
Interpreting recorded material. A teacher's book gives further suggestions
for use and some suggested interpretations of the sound sequences.

The N.A.S.A. game

Pfeiffer and Jones, *A handbook of structured experiences for human relations
training,* Vol. 1, University Associates Press.

Miscellaneous reading

A large number of articles and books relevant to the subject of *Discussions
that work* have been published in recent years. The six mentioned below
are ones which I have found particularly interesting and useful.

I. S. P. Nation, 'The combining arrangement: some techniques', *Modern
Language Journal,* March 1977.
Donn Byrne, 'Oral expression through visuals', *English Teaching Forum,*
11:4, Sep./Oct. 1973.
Alan Maley, 'The teaching of listening comprehension skills', *Modern
English Teacher* 6:3, 1978.
S. Rixon, 'The information gap and the opinion gap', *English Language
Teaching* 33:2, 1979.
Norman F. Davies, 'Oral fluency training and small groups', *English
Teaching Forum* 18:3, 1980.
J. Moffett, *A student-centered language arts curriculum,* Houghton-Mifflin,
1968.
This is about teaching English to young native speakers, but it is full of
insights, generalizations, suggestions and advice that are invaluable to
the foreign-language teacher as well. Very readable.

Index

Alibi 58
Associations 36
Categories 49
Character studies 43
Characteristics 38
Choosing candidates (a) 73
Choosing candidates (b) 79
Combining elements into a
  story 34
Combining versions 90
Comparing 48
Composing letters 98
Connecting pairs 33
Couples 84
Debates 105
Detecting differences 51
Dinner party 87
Doodles 39
Explanations 46
Features and functions 72
Finding connections 33
Finding things in common 35
Foreseeing results 45
Guessing games 27
Heirs 76
Ideas from a central theme 35

Implications and interpreta-
  tions 39
Interpreting pictures 40
Interpreting recorded mate-
  rial 40
Layout problems 80
Men from Mars 45
Odd man out 48
Picture differences 52
Picture-sequence 60
Planning projects 112
Priorities 67
Prisoners 77
Prize-winners 74
Publicity campaigns 108
Putting in order 60
Qualities 36
Rating 68
Sentence-sequence 65
Surveys 111
Survival games 70
Uses of an object 37
Victims 78
What will you need? 38
Zoo plan 81